Stories

of a rambler

and a gambler

by

Barney Carr

© 2021
Barney Carr hereby asserts his moral right to be identified as the author of "Stories of a rambler and a gambler"

*For Bridget, Brendan and Maureen,
who are now the owners of the
time and work that went into
this project*

CONTENTS:

CHAPTER 1: GROWING UP AND WORKING FOR UNCLE SAM................................ 7

CHAPTER 2: GOING BUSH 34

CHAPTER 3: IRELAND AND FIRST MARRIAGE 81

CHAPTER 4: BACK TO IRELAND AND MORE TRAVELS 125

CHAPTER 5: NEW FAMILY 154

**Hello Bridget and Brendan and Maureen.
I just want to get this written down, so if for any reason I am no longer in the land of the living, you will have some knowledge of me...**

CHAPTER 1 – GROWING UP AND WORKING FOR UNCLE SAM

Early years

I was born in 1940 in southwest Philadelphia, a working-class neighborhood with a mix of Irish, Italian and Polish immigrants mingled with the residents. I do not remember anything about the Second World War, and the first President I remember is President Harry Truman being elected in 1948. We had a small city row house, at 2523 South 62nd street, Philadelphia. I was the fifth and last child, and the only one born in a house owned by my parents. The other four were born in rented houses. I hope you can understand how difficult it was for your grandparents at that time. Your grandfather worked on the docks in Philadelphia for over thirty years. He had a third-grade education which he brought over with him when he emigrated from Ireland in his twenties, but I can honestly say he had a lot of wisdom. Your grandmother was born in Scotland and had an eighth-grade education so she could spell much better and write well. There is a whole book put together by my cousin John Feerick on our grandparents' migration from Scotland to Philadelphia, which I will pass on to you if you wish to read up on it.

Although our family did not have a big income, there were always some little ways to pick up a bit of pocket money. You could collect old newspapers and rags and take them up to the man who weighed them and paid you. Then there was Friday and Saturday night, when you could make the rounds of the local pubs with your shoeshine box and gear and offer to shine shoes. There was plenty of work around the area at the time for people who were old enough to work in industry. So, the pubs were busy with local lads out for the night. I charged twenty-five cents for a shine. I used to be able to bring home sometimes as much as three or four dollars plus. At the time it was more money than I knew how to spend, so it was given over to my parents.

In 1950, the Korean War began. My shoeshine business went down the tubes, as a lot of my customers got drafted into the army. My brother Eddie was the first of my two brothers to get drafted. He spent 11 months in Korea, and my brother John, even though he was two years younger, got his draft notice six months later. He spent all his active duty in the States. It was not good for my shoeshine business.

The family lived in the south-west Philly house until I was twelve or thirteen, and then we moved or migrated to what they called the suburbs, a move up. My aunt moved out to the same suburb, which was called Sharon Hill. She had a son who was a year younger than me and we were in the same grade at school. The reason we were in the same grade was that I spent two years in second grade.

The church there was in the Holy Spirit Parish. It was a church that was getting more and more migrants from the city. I got the idea of selling Sunday newspapers to people as they left the church after Mass every Sunday. I think I was the only 12-year-old, and it was a bit scary to order a lot of Sunday papers by myself which cost twenty-five cents each at the time. I told my friend and we decided to do it. We ordered 75 Sunday newspapers and we were sold out, with three Masses still ahead. The partnership split, and we each took it every other week. It was great for a kid to make fifteen dollars every two weeks. I did have to get up very early Sunday morning and get the papers set up.

The one thing I learned from the business was not to be afraid to do things by yourself. If you think of a good business and if there is any way you can do it yourself, do it yourself. I had to watch my ex-partner make that good money every other week. That money, plus whatever I could pick up cutting grass, shoveling snow or gathering and selling trash

- that was worth something. It kept me going enough that I did not, for the most part, have to get money from my parents.

When I turned sixteen, I bought a truck. It was a 1939 Ford three-quarter ton van truck. I enjoyed the truck for fun, and somebody always had a small job for me and the truck. I did graduate from high school, though it took me a long time - I left for a year and worked at some menial jobs in a department store. It was awful. When the time came for the next school year to start, my brother Eddie told me if I did not go back to school that year I would never go back, so I registered at the school and was admitted. I had two more years to do. I was not a good student as I did not like school. I put in just enough days to get through. A few other students and I had to go to summer school for failing a couple of classes. It ruined my summer, as I could not get a steady job to pick up money. But once I got into the last year, there was no way I was going to quit.

I was very grateful to my brother Eddie for talking to me about how important school was. I think I was the oldest student in the class of 1960. My mother and father came to my graduation, and I remember her saying 'you finally made it'! I was the only one of the four brothers to graduate from high school. That high school diploma opened a lot of doors for me. My only sister, who was one year older, graduated from a private high school in 1957. She was a very good scholar. We (brothers and sister) were blessed with a loving family, good neighbors and friends, who would help you up if you fell, and try to catch you if they saw you falling. It is something I tried to do the rest of my life. Two months after graduation I went to sea on an oil tanker, but that will be my next segment.

Early Years

Barney in Second Grade, 1948

Barney in Fourth Grade, 1950

Barney with cousins, at Jersey Shore, 1952

Barney's graduation photo, 1960

Going to sea
Happy seven-month birthday, Bridget, June 2nd.

Life at sea for this young sailor began August 1960. The sea was very good to me. I was having a few problems as a youth, and it got me off the streets, where I could have had serious problems down the road. Work on the ship put a bit of a jingle in my pocket. I spent two and a half years working tankers up and down the east coast of the USA, and a few runs down to South America.

My first ship was the Atlantic Trader, and the captain was Thomas DeTemple - I did not know at the time that he was a great captain, as it was my first merchant ship. As time went on, I found out just how good he was. One trip we made, I believe it was from Texas to somewhere up in New England, we ran smack into a hurricane that we had to fight our way through. I remember Captain DeTemple spending four days on the bridge, sleeping on a cot in the chart room. The ship was one that was built during the Second World War and a lot of them did break in half in bad weather. This one was known as a jumbo T-2 tanker. It went into a shipyard in the fifties, and it was cut in half and another set of tanks was welded in. It was a great ship with a great crew and captain.

In January or February 1963, I got a draft notice for the US army. They wanted me to report for military duty on the 12th of March. I was down in South America at the time I got the notice, posted to my parents' address. The ship I was working on came back to Texas and I did not see my name on the list to be relieved, so I thought maybe they forgot about me. But we went from there up to Boston, Mass., which was where the list came in and my name was on there - so I got off and reported to the US army for two years' service. That is for the next page.

Life in the Army
Hello Bridget, Brendan and Maureen.

I reported on the 12th of March 1963. Spent the first eight weeks in Fort Dix, New Jersey. The closest I must have been to home for a long time. After basic training, I was assigned to Fort Belvoir, Virginia. I only stayed there for two weeks, and then got ordered to report to 344th transportation company at Fort Story, Virginia. It was right there at the

Cape Hendry lighthouse, right across the bay from Cape Charles lighthouse leading into the Chesapeake Bay. This was an amphibious army company, with what they called at the time LARCs (Light Amphibious Recovery Craft).

The first fellow to greet me there was from Sligo, Ireland. He was the company clerk. It was an encounter that had a very good effect on my life. His time was getting short (soon to be released from active duty). We had a chat, and he asked me if I would be interested in working in the orderly room. I thought he was looking at somebody else's file, as I was hardly ever in an office, other than to apply for a job or for reasons of discipline. But sure enough, he was looking at my file. What I did notice in my short time in the army was that the clerks did not do KP (kitchen patrol) or guard duty, and did not have to wait in line for chow. I said I would try, and next thing I was going to typing school for half of every day for six weeks to learn the keyboard. At that time there were no electric typewriters, at least not in the army. All manual, just punch away. I learnt the job, he was released, and I was number two clerk. The number one clerk was a lad from California, a bit flighty, but at the time he was still number one.

In the office at the time, the company commander was a Captain Joseph E. Hines III from Louisiana, who spoke very good English until he got excited and reverted to the old Louisiana slang. There was the first sergeant, number one clerk and me in that office. The company also had one lieutenant and two second lieutenants, plus a warrant officer in charge of maintenance for the LARC. The officers were looked after by the company commander (CO) and the first sergeant E-8 looked after all the other sergeants (E- 5 thru E-7). The company clerk looked after all the rest, known as grunts. We were short on personnel, but after a while, we started getting transfers from battalions, to make up our roster and for other personnel changes.

As time went on, I could see these changes happening, but did not know where they were coming from or for what purpose. You must realize this was the early sixties and the Vietnam War was starting to build up. In mid-1964, we acquired a new company CO and first sergeant. The new CO was Captain Thomas O'Donovan. He was all army and went to all the right army schools. He was one good soldier to serve under. The company was a combat-ready company and we were supposed to be able to load up and move out in 24 hours, with all our equipment and personnel. By then I knew our company was destined for Viet Nam.

We started going through all kinds of drills and other war games. The one I do remember well was we had a planned invasion of an uninhabited Island in North Carolina, about a 6-hour truck ride from Fort Story. My job was to load up all my equipment that would be needed to get the company morning report typed up and sent to battalion headquarters. After a day of packing, we were on the road early next day, and camped out that night near a beach. Early next morning we packed our personal duffel bags, and a day's rations to make a beach landing. This was in the winter and it was cold and raining while all this was going on. On Smith Island the first thing that was set up was the chow tent with their pot-bellied stoves - that was a warm place. After we got the orderly room set up and the morning report sent out, I found my way to the chow tent and got some shut-eye next to a nice warm pot-belly stove. We stayed camped there for a few days, then packed up and headed back to Fort Story. That was a dry run for the trip to Viet Nam.

The first sergeant decided to shift the number one clerk to another company that was not going anywhere, so now I was the number one clerk with an assistant. The first allotment for rank that came down from battalion was given to me, which made me a specialist E-4. I was now making one hundred and twenty-one dollars a month. When I was working the ships, I was making five hundred a month. I was still glad to serve my country though, and it was only for two years, so I could do that standing on my head. As my time was getting short the army sent me my relief, a schoolteacher from up in New England somewhere. He was a great guy with a lot of smarts, who had no trouble fitting right in.

I was released from active duty on March 11, 1965. The company shipped out to Vietnam in May of that year. I did not find out what kind of losses they took. I do know I knew a lot of them, and they were some great soldiers. They were deployed to Cam Ranh Bay, Vietnam. I got over to Cam Ranh Bay later on a merchant ship, but all the ones I knew had finished their tour and had been sent home. The company was still there, but I did not know anyone. The army was a great experience and I would recommend it to anyone. I met some great people who I enjoyed spending time with.

Race relations in the sixties

Before moving on, I would like to expand a bit more on the US army in the sixties. The army was integrated after the Second World War, when there was just one military for all races. Being stationed at an army base in the south was quite interesting. On the base everything was integrated. As soon as you left the base, things were different, up in headquarters platoon where there were about twenty of us in the barracks. There was only one black soldier (Ernie Ford), he was the armourer which is the one who takes care of all the company weapons. He was what we called a lifer (one who reenlists and makes a life out of the army). He is the one who kept my weapon well oiled. A big fear every soldier has is to hear 'click' when they fire their weapon, and when you know you are in some deep muck.

There, I had two other soldiers that I spent a lot of time with off base. One was from Virginia and the other from Michigan. Both were merchant seaman like me who got drafted. We would go off base and stop in a saloon and do our thing, but we could never take Ernie to the pub with us, as black people did not associate with white people in public places in Virginia in the sixties. We could bring a white killer and a rapist into the bar, but not Ernie (who was a fine gentleman and a good soldier), only because he was black. That bothered me then, but I was not brave enough to stand up and protest against the injustice which was in effect at the time; off base I just accepted things as they were at the time.

Things have improved since then and are moving in the right direction. We even have had a US President who is a man of colour. The biggest benefit from Obama is not whether you agreed with him or not, the greatest benefit is the message it sent to the rest of the world about the United States of America - that it could elect a man of colour to the highest office of the land. I believe the lesson to be learnt from this time period is that it is the duty of the majority government to give the minority access to all government benefits and the freedom to integrate. I do believe in an inclusive society which is much better than an exclusive society in the long term. There are people in many countries who are in the minority, and no way could they ever see one of their own getting elected to the highest office in their government. That's a very positive message that the USA sent to the world. It said a lot about the USA today.

Anyway, after I finished my military draft, I was a civilian again, but was soon to be back on ships - in fact 11 days after my release from active duty, I was back on a tanker sailing the deep blue sea. That's another story though. I will try and do an hour a day if I can. I do hope you enjoy it. Later.

Back to Ships
Hello again!

I got out of the army on the 11th March 1965. I had my army duffel bag, with all my army-issued clothes. I put the bag up in the attic in my sister's house in Moylan, Pennsylvania. I did not stay there for long. After 11 days, I got bored and went back to work on the oil tankers again. I already had Able-Bodied Seaman (ABS) papers with my lifeboat ticket, but there was not much work in an AB position at the oil company where I was employed. You needed one year of sea time to sit the AB test by law, as ships were only allowed to carry one AB with a green ticket - where the test was taken with only one year of sea time. After three years of sea time, you automatically get the full ticket. The test was taken down at 2nd and Chestnut St. in Philadelphia, where there was a coast-guard office that tested seamen. I do not know if it is still there or not.

After I got my AB ticket with the oil company where I was working, at the time they were cutting back on ships, and I got some AB work, but not much. I found out through the seaman's grapevine that they were taking job applications at the Brooklyn Navy Yard at 58th and 1st Ave in Brooklyn, New York. I went up there and got hired as AB the same day, to join up with a ship in Adak, Alaska – it did not take me long to pack the old sea bag. This was quite different, as it was the first time that I would work a freighter. It did not take me too long before I got things sorted and back on the high seas, going from point A to B.

Army and Navy

Brother Eddie in Korea, 1951-2

Barney on oil tanker, 1960-61

Military service, 1963

Hard life in the Army!

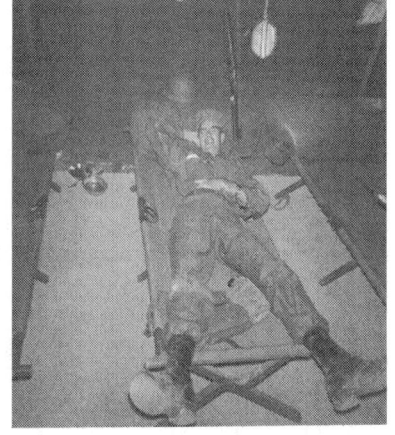

The ship was another Second World War ship that they built a lot of out on the west coast. They called them the Victory Ships or the Old Stick Ships. Again, they were great ships, just like the T-2 tankers. They have one Victory Ship as a museum tied up down in Tampa, Florida. I got a chance to see it and it brought back some fond memories. You can google Victory Ships and T-2 tankers, they have a lot of info on those ships, as they played a big part in the Second World War. This was all before containers or roll on roll off ships (roros). They used booms to load and discharge all cargo, that's why they were called Stick Ships. The name of the ship was the 'Craig'. I stayed on that ship for a while, most of the time out in the Far East. That is when there were a lot of ships delivering goods to Vietnam and other ports in the Far East. The ship went under the command of the office in Yokohama, Japan.

I spent the best part of three years out in the Far East sailing about. I was known as a Far East sailor working out of Yokohama, Japan. I really liked the Far East then, and it was 39 years before I got back there, and I found out I still liked the Far East. There is one story that happened on that ship that is worth telling. We sailed back from the Far East through Europe, where we picked up a lot of older military explosives that had to be reworked back in the States; these were stored on a Greek Island, Crete, and at the Greek port of Athens, and also at two other ports in Italy and Portugal. We made one more port up in Norway before heading across the Atlantic. (We got 10 percent added pay for carrying bombs). It was a great hardworking crew. We had a great poker game also. Anyway, the chief electrician had some money problems (debts) with the second electrician. A few days into the crossing, the chief electrician went missing at sea. It was the first or second day out of Norway. I was working the 12-4 watch (midnight until 4am and noon until 4pm). It was a watch I always liked. I enjoyed how peaceful it was between midnight and 4 in the morning. Well, those four or five days remaining to get to New York were long ones. All the crew pretty much knew what happened, but nobody was talking to anybody other than what was necessary.

When we arrived in New York, the federal marshals came on board. It was not too long before the second electrician was taken off the ship. What he said happened was, they were up on the bow and the chief electrician made sexual advances on him and he, the second electrician, threw him overboard. This was not believable. I talked to the electrician when I saw him in a bar in Brooklyn, a while after they took him off the ship. He did not do any jail time, but they did pull his seaman's papers, so he lost his livelihood and would never be able to work on another American Flag Ship - a big loss for anyone, but some people would say not enough. What they took into consideration was the long confinement of being on the ship, which I find hard to believe. It was nothing but money. He also owed me money, which I told him to forget about. That was the only crime on all the ships I spent time on.

Easter Island

Hello! The Wyandot is one of the most amazing ships I have ever had the pleasure to crew. It was a large five-hold cargo ship. The thing that made this ship special was, it had a 200-ton boom on there. There was no other ship in the world that had that kind of lifting power. I looked it up now and found out it is mothballed in a bone yard. It is being kept ready to be brought out in an emergency in short notice. I do not know if they equipped another ship to replace it. It was 1966 or 1967 or maybe some of both years. I joined the ship somewhere on the east coast. Overall, I think it had the best sailors of any ship I sailed on up until then. We sailed south to the Panama Canal, where we loaded 8 thousand, 55-gallon barrels of asphalt and tar. The weight of each was somewhere around 600 pounds. We also loaded anchor buoys for large ships to make fast to where there was no pier. We needed the big boom for the buoys.

We sailed out of Balboa, Panama heading into the South Pacific. We were at sea for a while. What we were looking for was Easter Island. It is quite a famous island that has been studied, but there are still many unanswered questions. The asphalt and tar were for an air strip that the Chilean Government wanted to put in there. The buoys were for visiting ships to make fast to, as there were no piers there. Before we got there, they had two visits a year by Chilean ships to bring in supplies and people, and take people back. I do not think there was much to take back to the mainland which was thousands of miles away. When I got there, it had a woman's penal colony and a leprosy colony. They had a medical building, and some nuns with a priest there. I got to chat with the priest who had spent twenty-five years there. His name was Father Sebastian.

I did not spend much time ashore there, as there was a lot of work to get done. We were at anchor and had to unload 8 thousand heavy barrels. There were no stevedores down there, so the crew had to work all the gear for unloading the ship. Let's get started, open the hatches. We had about twenty deck personnel to do the job. We worked as many hours as we wanted. It was a bit dicey down in the holds, with the ship rolling and the heavy round barrels. We had to get into the center so we could either net them, or use a special barrel rig that hooked on the edges of the barrel. We could put four in the net and three with the grippers. Anyhow it took a long time to get them all off the ship and onto the barges to be taken ashore. There was a construction crew from Chile who took charge once they reached the barge. We were there about three months with unloading cargo and laying the buoys. We lifted the buoys and positioned them over the stern of a big barge and lowered it down into the water, and we made the anchor fast to the stern of the barge to locate the buoy where it was best suited for future ships coming in to make fast to it.

With most of the cargo unloaded, I decided to check out the island. It was an experience for myself and my shipmate from Cuba. We made it ashore, and they gave us some horses to ride around the island. We rode into this one little settlement and all the people came out to see us and they had bandages all over their bodies, and they just begged us for whatever we had. The only thing I had was some cigarettes, which I was glad to pass on and get out of there. We made our way to what I would think was the main village, and the ladies were very glad to see us. This could have been a fantasy, but it was really happening. I was asleep the first night and it rained hard and the roof started to leak. The fine lady got out of bed, went up on the roof and fixed it. I thought to myself, where else could this happen. A strange thing happened when we were ashore, the sea came up and the ship pulled anchor and went out to sea. We did not know how long the sea was going to stay up and the ship stay out at sea. It did not take long before I figured that there was not too much over there to eat, and what was there was not just given away freely. What they did have was a lot of bananas, real small ones but sweet. My Cuba shipmate had brought over a lot of Hershey chocolate bars. I saw him and told him not to give them all away until we see the ship come back. So anyway, I did spend three days ashore there. It was very interesting. It's an interesting place to read about. I have not tried to google it though.

Another thing happened when I was at Easter Island. A young man on the ship had a ham radio. We were in the mess hall and he asked me if there was anybody I wanted to call, and if he got hold of somebody close, he would ask them to call. I gave him my sister's number and sure enough he got hold of somebody with a ham radio in New Hampshire, and he called my sister collect, using my name. So my sister got this collect phone call out of the blue from New Hampshire from me. She did not know where I was, but New Hampshire was the last place she expected, as she knew I was on a ship somewhere. She did accept the call and we had a chat. The only thing she had to do was say 'over' when she was finished talking and I had to do the same. Even today, in emergencies, those radios are still very useful when all the towers and electricity are out, but I do not think too many people are still into them, with all the computer things happening. Barney.

Well, I still have got over 40 years to write about. The next ship was a new ship, a roro ship. Roll on roll off ship. Something new at the time. Now that's all they have is roro and container ships.

Sailing the Far East

During the time I spent sailing around the South China Sea, I got to most of the ports out there. The ones I recall mostly are Subic Bay, Philippines, Okinawa, and Kaoh Siung in Taiwan. What was known as the best port in the Far East was Bangkok, Thailand. I always enjoyed Yokohama, Japan or what we called Yokodo. I got back to the States, I don't know what year, and they gave me a survey ship to work on - that did not last long. We went out for months and went around in circles.

The interesting thing that happened on that ship was we had some scientists on there and one got sick, so a mate, myself and another AB launched a life-boat to take him ashore at this little British West Indian Island - it was Cat Island, which is the same island that Sidney Poitier comes from. Anyway, the ship was on one side of the island and we landed on the other side as that is where its air-strip was. As we brought the life boat up on the beach, there was an old fisherman there working on his boat! He looked at us as we were wearing life vests and he looked at the lifeboat and was amazed at the boat we had. He asked us if we came all the way across the ocean. We got the scientist sorted, and picked up a case of beer and went back to the ship. I only made one trip on that ship as it did not suit me.

The next job they sent me on was a much better trip, in fact one that I remember fondly. I remember it was May and it was just a delivery. The ship was in what we called the bone yard down in Wilmington, North Carolina. It had been laid up for a while. It was another 2nd World War Ship - another google for you, an LST landing ship.

So, I had done a couple of Transpacific trips before and was thinking to put in about thirty days, we would deliver the ship to Korea and I could get back and enjoy some time down the Jersey shore. The engineers got the big diesel engines going and we got the deck gear together and off we sailed, heading for the Panama Canal. About six days later we were going through the Panama Canal. When we get to the Pacific side, they found some cracks in the deck and the freeboard. Into the shipyard in Panama we went to be patched up, which took about a week. We also loaded up with cargo for Vietnam and we headed out into the Pacific, going to Hawaii, I think, when we hit a bit of bad weather and there were more cracks, so we headed up to California Long Beach shipyard for some more repairs. After the repairs we headed out into the Pacific again, this time heading for Guam. We had yet more problems, docked in Hawaii and back into the shipyard to get some welding done. There was no way that ship would ever pass coastguard inspection. Nobody cared because the ship was not coming back to the States again. You must understand when I took this job, I was thinking a month. We had great officers and crew on that ship. Every shipyard and port we had a lot of fun, so since we had not made it to Guam, we had enough fuel to make it to the Philippines - but that did not happen, we did eventually make it to Guam and got some more repairs. From there we made it to the Philippines.

It was interesting when we got there as they completely discharged all our cargo and backloaded us with cargo for Nam. The word going around the ship was that the cargo that they unloaded there was good and valuable, and the cargo they backloaded us with was not worth so much. Makes you think how much value they put on the officers and crew. We made a couple of shuttle runs from Nam to Naha and back before we headed north to Korea. We finally sailed into Pusan and it was Christmas Eve, 1966, and we got paid off. The Koreans could not get on there fast enough.

So now we have reached the time from 5th Jan 1968 when I took a bad hit in Vietnam, until I got back to the Far East 39 years later, which I will go through next. **With love, Barney.**

The life-changing accident

My last working ship was the USNS COMET T-LSU-7. I joined the ship in mid to late 1967. Cannot remember where. It was a roll-on roll-off ship (RoRo). It was the newest ship I ever worked. RORO at the time was new to merchant shipping. I cannot remember if the crew's quarters were much of an improvement on the older ships. I am sure if there was some big differences I would remember, like having your own focal (room).

This is beginning to be a difficult one to write because of how life-changing it was for me. It was a good ship and we were making short trips from Okinawa to Vietnam, so we were in port a lot. Being a roro ship, it had to have a dock that could accommodate the ship. The US had built what was needed at a dock in Saigon and other ports in Vietnam. We ran mostly into Saigon. There was this port on the Mekong River - Knob Bay - about 10 miles south of Saigon, a little village with a few bars and the prettiest ladies. The life of sailors!

After a few trips back and forth to Vietnam, we went straight into Saigon, and I was working the midnight to 8 am gangway watch. As it was Saigon, we also had a security watch. My shipmate, who was from somewhere in Texas, was on security and was very interested in Knob Bay, which is the village. He wanted me to show him around down there, so we both got off watch at 8am. He had a motorcycle on board ship which he would use while in port. This was all new to me. I have never seen anyone do that before. Just another first. So we headed off on his motorcycle, I would think about 9am, heading toward Knob Bay. My shipmate was from Texas somewhere. He did come to visit me in Pennsylvania, perhaps a year after the mishap. My sister talked to him more than I did. I think I just wanted to put ships behind me and move on. I was working the pizza shop at the time and working a lot of hours.

Anyway, we got down there and had a few beers, and started to head back to the ship. I would think we were a bit tired after being up all night and we had to get back to work at midnight again. On the way back I was driving the motorcycle, and the road was bad, with a lot of big potholes. I was motoring along dodging all the holes, and what looked like a French jeep was speeding down the road coming towards us - he was doing the same as me, going from side to side - and we smashed head on. I can still see his face about six inches from me.

The only thing I can remember is a split second view of some very old lady pouring kerosene on my leg while I was lying on the road, whether or not that really happened, I can't tell. The accident happened on January 5th, and on January 6th, I was taken into 24th Evacuation Hospital, Long Binh, Republic of Vietnam. Where I spent the night of the 5th January is still a mystery to me.

I remember the first doctor I talked to; his name was Doctor Rodriguez. He told me he had tried to put my knee back together, but it was just shattered. It was then I think that I had my first seizure, so there was some brain damage there. When I woke up again, the side bars were up on my bed. What I do remember though is seeing my leg in a cast. I thought I had broken my leg, and that I would be back on the ship in six weeks. I was never laid up before, so I thought this was just something that I would get through in no time at all. I would think that I was on some pretty heavy drugs during that time.

I spent ten days in that field hospital in Vietnam, and was then flown off to the Clark Air Force base in the Philippines. While I was there, they found out that my right hip was also very badly damaged, and I would have to be put into traction. I had a pin going through my hip, and pulley rigs over the outside of the bed with a twenty-pound weight hanging off it. I also had a ten-pound weight hanging off my right foot. The bed was tilted about thirty degrees so the weight would work better, plus a cast on my left arm and left leg with the knee destroyed.

It was there that I got a staph infection in my knee, and they had a drip with the liquid keeping the knee wet all the time, the infection was extremely painful. I stayed in that bed like that for about three months – that's a long time without a shower or being out of bed. Good fortune was that they had some good drugs (morphine). Until this day, I still say it is the most wonderful drug in the world. I was getting injected every four hours, and then passing out for two hours before waking up with the pain. They would then come by and give me a pill which was not much help. I would lay there, just waiting for the injection again.

I remember the ward I was in was filled up with six or eight beds. I was the only one in there who had all my limbs. You've got to remember this was January, 1968, when the Viet Cong (the combatants of the other side) were doing the TET offensive, which a lot of people said turned the war around. There were a lot of US casualties at the time. One thing I do remember a bit is a visit from Rosemary Clooney, who was one of your grandmother's favourite entertainers. She came by my bed, and I think I was not in the best form - and she asked me if I would give her a phone number of somebody over in the States that she could call up. I told her my mother was one of her favourite fans. She did call my mother down in the Villas, New Jersey, and from what I heard they talked for about half-an-hour. My mother was very surprised to get a call from Rosemary Clooney.

Return to the States and rehab –
Happy 4th of July, Barney.
Hello again. . . I would think the hospital in the Philippines was packed out when I was over there, with the TET offensive going strong, so somebody made the decision to ship me over to San Francisco. That is where they had a US public health hospital or seaman's hospital. I do

not know the date, but I think I was in Clark Air Force Hospital for about three months. I will never forget the plane trip over. I was drugged, but I remember the plane being packed with stretchers stacked on top of each other. It was very painful all the way. I remember saying to myself when I got to the hospital in San Francisco, that I was not moving anymore until I can walk.

When I first got to San Francisco, I remember the doctor who looked at my leg saying 'that's nice'. I was put in isolation because of the infection. It was a ward down at the end of a long corridor that had about twelve or more beds in there. They started giving me a shot once a day, and right away the infection and pain started to subside, which was a great feeling. The doctors used to come into the ward and put on their yellow coats, then discard them on the way out. We were treated well in there as far as being kept clean and fed. I do not remember just how long I was in there, but I was gradually improving and sitting in a wheelchair and going to rehab in the morning and afternoon.

I do not know what the infection was or where I picked it up. It was either in Vietnam or Philippines, but it was a bad one. I do not know what drug they gave me to fight it. I would think it was something toxic and heavy. It was several months and I still was not on my feet, just able to manoeuver from the bed to the wheelchair. It was great just to be able to get down to the mess hall, and pull the chair up to a special table and eat a meal.

My recovery started moving pretty good after that, and I was feeling much better, as I was off all drugs except the one for the seizures. The last month or so I was able to get to a pay phone and make a few phone calls. By now my leg had fused, so it was the way it is today, and the hip must have healed also. I was down in the physical therapy room, where they had these walking bars, and I got up and took a few steps - this is after being there for about three months. I remember when the doctor came around to visit the next day, I asked him when I could leave, and he said when I can walk. I said how about Friday, and he said ok. The next three days I was on crutches prancing around. When Friday came, somebody found some clothes for me, I do not remember where from, because I had not worn any clothes for about six months. I remember them giving me a bag, with one shoe in it and some other stuff. Somebody in the hospital must have booked a flight from San Francisco to Philadelphia.

Through all this I will always be eternally indebted to all the wonderful caregivers who helped me get to where I was able to get back on my feet and walk. I was now going to be an outpatient. Looking back now I can see how all three hospitals moved me along in some difficult situations. The field hospital in Vietnam was just to keep me breathing and to give me a bit of strength to move me to Clark Air Force Base. Clark Air Force Base let me rest, and gave me a chance for the bones to heal. San Francisco was to cure the infection, reduce the drugs and give me physical therapy. I was now able to fly across country alone, but on crutches.

Back to Philadelphia

Hello again. . . here I am, getting ready to leave the hospital with all my worldly possessions. I know I had one shoe and a belt, but I cannot remember anything else. I am sure they had to cut the rest of the clothes off me after the accident. When you are living on a ship you do not tend to accumulate too many worldly possessions, as there is not that much room. I do not know what happened to the things I had on the ship.

There was another seaman leaving the hospital the same day and he offered to help me get to the airport and checked in. I do not remember too much about that. We are talking over forty years ago. What I do remember is arriving in Philadelphia and getting off the plane, and having four people meet me. It was my three brothers and Jack Shields, who was a good friend of my brother Eddie and myself. This was all before they had these tunnels leading right into the plane, so I came down the stairs on my crutches. I think I was the last one off, because I was not so quick on my feet. I was in bad shape, but one thing was for sure, nobody was going to take advantage of me - with that crew I had around me, whatever I needed they would sort out for me. It was a very good feeling that I still remember fondly and with a smile.

I think we went to my brother Joseph's house, where we took some drink and I had a pretty bad seizure. His wife was a nurse, so she handled things. I continued to take seizures when I drank too much or got too tired. I was on meds for the disorder, which I believed worked well, so long as I stayed away from the devil drink. My Able Body Seaman days were gone forever.

My business venture

Hello again. . . My stay back in PA was a good one. I stayed at my sister's house. I do not remember how long it was before an offer came up to buy a pizza shop in Ridley Township, Delaware, Co., Pennsylvania. It was brought to me from a good friend of my brother Eddie. He was an accountant who used to work for the Internal Revenue, but had left and got a job with an accountancy firm. He was doing income taxes for some pizza shops, so he was aware of what was happening with the finances of the business.

It was a Greek fellow who was selling his shop. He had been in partnership with his brothers in the business, but then went out on his own. He was asking $35,000 for the business. Having no knowledge of the pizza business I had no way of knowing just how much business there was there, so that is where the accountant came into play. He was a friend of the family, and from the same neighborhood in Southwest Philly. He went on to university, and not too many from that time and neighborhood went on to higher education. There was one supplier to the business who would not take payment in cash, the one who sold paper supplies to the shop, so my accountant figured out that if he was using that many paper plates, he was selling a lot of pies.

I was lucky that all the years I spent at sea, I had managed to put up some money. I had about $12,000 put up, which was a lot in 1968, so I decided to put my life savings into this pizza business. The Greek guy was a lot of help to me, which I can understand, as he was holding the balance of the loan - he wanted me to succeed so he could get paid. It was a good lump for a down payment. I also got access to a $3,000 loan from the bank if I needed more cash. It so happened that I did not need the bank money.

Money, money, money, work, work, work

The accountant's name was Mike Concannon. There were a lot of Irish names in the old hood. I would just like to make it known that people sometimes come into your life for a reason that you may never know. Mike made my life different for the better, I believe. That is something that we will never know for sure. I like the old saying, doors open and doors close. One door closed on me and another opened. I did not have to spend too long in the cold hallway. He was my accountant until I sold the business to my brother Eddie. The main thing he told me was not to deposit more money in the bank than I was claiming on my taxes.

Well here I am, no savings left and a business to attend to, and I owe 23,000 dollars. Let's get to work and count the money later. The pizza shop opened at 4pm and stayed open until 1am, and 2am on weekends. The first thing Fred the Greek taught me was the recipe for the tomato sauce (the secret recipe) - everything is in the sauce. The customers did not know the shop was changing hands. Fred had had problems with the health inspector there, though I only found that out soon after I took over. I would say Fred stayed around maybe at the most ten hours. I learned to operate the oven, and got to know all the suppliers. The staff he left me were good enough.

It was not too long before I had to hire people. I had three part-time oven men and waitresses, one during the week and two on weekends. Altogether I had ten or twelve people working for me, all part-time. I was the only full-time worker as most of the business was deliveries. I used to charge 25 cents and 50 cents. The money started rolling in and I made all my payments on time. I would waken about noon and get to the shop about 2.30 or 3pm and get things set up. I had one kid that was always on time to clean the place up. I would do every job in the shop except mop the floor. I would be able to get out of there about a half-hour after we closed. It was a long day for me, but being busy it went by fast. There was an after-hours club right behind the shop, where I used to go and have a few beers. I do not think I ever got back home until at least 5 am, to sleep and get up and do it again. The shop was closed on Tuesdays, so I had a chance to catch up on some things. It was strange because, come Wednesday, I would be just as tired as I was on Monday, as I was running around on Tuesday - so I would tell myself next week, I will just rest which I would do. Come

Wednesday I felt rested, but not happy not getting things done... (Crazy I know.).

Anyway, the pile of money kept getting bigger and bigger. I stayed at the business for about two and half years. Got everyone paid off and had a nice stash. My brother Eddie, who worked with Boeing airlines making helicopters for Vietnam, was laid off, as the war was winding down about that time. He was on his last week of unemployment payments when he took over the business, which worked out good for all of us. He was now married and had two young kids. He started making the money and paid off his house. I was not about, so I do not know what kind of toll it took on him with the worries of a business.

Cross-country trip

I could have stayed there and made more, but I thought I cannot stay in one place. This is over forty years ago, and I think I am still the same, though the moves now are getting harder. I keep making them though. When I left the east coast for California, I had about one hundred thousand put away, including the money owed to me by my brother Eddie, whom I sold the business to. I travelled across the States and got to Reno, Nevada, and I was going to spend a night there. I ended up staying there for three months.

I am trying to remember what I was doing in Reno, Nevada for three months. On the trip out west, I stopped in Michigan to touch base with one of my army buddies to see how he was doing. When I left the east coast, as I said, I had one hundred thousand, which today would be like half a million with today's money, so I was feeling comfortable money wise. He was back working on the ships out of Alpine, Michigan and was not going anywhere. We used to kid him when we called him a pond sailor. This was in the middle of winter, so there was not too much work up there for him. Anyway, I was glad I got a chance to stop by and see him.

The trip out across Nebraska and into Nevada was a fun drive in my 1970 deuce and a quarter Buick. (225). It was a great machine, the best new machine I ever bought. The 1969 Chrysler Newport was the worst new or used car I ever bought. I was nervous even taking it around the block. I did not keep it long, as it was just a bad machine. I could not bring myself to sell it to anyone I knew, so I just chopped it up. When you have a bad machine and you sell it, you just pass the problem on, you do not cure it - and I think there was no cure for that machine. It's funny now, every time I get to an old car show and auction like Hershey, where there are hundreds of old cars, I look for that same 1969 Chrysler Newport, and I have not been able to find one. I am sure somebody has got one put up and is still dealing with the problems, but I have not seen any. What I always say about machines is, if they were good new, they are good 30 years later, and if they were bad new, they are still bad 30 years later.

Anyway, it was a fun trip driving across country in the winter going the northern route. Going across Wyoming on Interstate 80 in Laramie, I was laid up for three days as the road was closed due to snow. I did enjoy the three days there though, in that big university town. When I got to Reno, I was put up in a hotel with a good restaurant, that did a great Spanish omelette. I was not doing too much, just looking at different businesses - you see, now I was a proven businessman. I also spent a bit of time in the casinos and got familiar with the way things work there. They also got to know me, it's always a two-way street, if anybody thinks differently, they've got their head where the sun doesn't shine. This was all before Atlantic City opened its casinos.

La-La land

In the hotel bar I got to know a chap from Dublin, who was over there working as a waiter, and making a fair buck at it. He had spent some time down in La-La land (Los Angeles), so I picked his brain a bit about what was happening there. What I do remember about Reno is, I got to see Muhammed Ali, the greatest fighter, up in Lake Tahoe against the Canadian, who was a great puncher but also took a lot of punches. At the time I was not that sure about Ali, as to whether he could take a good punch. After that fight I was more of a believer in him. This was the second fight after he got his license back for his stand on the Vietnam War. He lost some of his best years as a fighter because of his stance, which I had no problem with. The other side of that coin is that

I believe his years as a fighter were extended, as I believe fighters only have so many tough fights in them. (More on boxing when we talk about my days as a fight promoter down in the jungles of Central America). Anyway, after three months in Reno, myself and Tom Harris, the Dubliner, were off to La-La land.

The trip down to La-La land was a long one, for some reason I remember a lot of night-driving over the San Bernardino mountains. I remember running into some late snow, and I was the only car on the road going over the mountain. I was sure glad to get over them. Reno is actually more to the west than la-la land.

When we got to Los Angeles, Tom knew his way around, and we got an apartment where he got himself a waiter's job. He had connections out there as far as waiter work went. I looked for locations to open another pizza shop. It did not take long, and I found one in Santa Ana in Orange County. It was close by where the apartment was. I went shopping for some suppliers and equipment for the shop. On my way out, I had stopped in Wisconsin to check out the cheese market, and made some connections there for cheese deliveries. It was interesting setting everything up, but also more expensive than I was expecting. I eventually got it all together. One lad who worked for me back east wanted to come out to work for me in California, so I gave him a job and he and his wife came west. He was a big expense, but he was also a very honest and good worker. It was not too long before Tom Harris decided to leave for Palm Springs, where he had an older lady who was his friend for a long time, and I think she used to help him out if he found himself in a hole.

I do not know how long I was out there when my brother Joe came out to join me. It was after he had a bad breakup with his wife. I was glad to see him, and he was a big help to me. Business was not going too well, and I was getting a bit tired of counting my money every month and having less than I did the month before. I did buy another shop which sold fish and chips, and I added pizza to the menu, which went well as I got to know a bit about the fish and chip business. I was starting to spread myself thin, with the two shops though, one just about breaking even, with the other losing money every month. My brother

Joe pretty much looked after the fish and chip shop and we got a new flat between the two shops.

We found a nice pub, a lot like Cheers, with some real characters. I would think that's also what the other customers thought about myself and Joe. The name of the place was the Phone Booth - wherever that came from, I do not know - it was not a big place and did not serve food. Milt was the owner who worked the late shift, so he was the one me and Joe got to know best. Vince, his partner, worked the day shift, except one day a week when they changed, so they both knew all the customers and the cash flow. They were both true blue bar-keepers with a lot of experience in the trade. What Milt used to do was when some ladies came in, he would buy them a drink and then think whose tab he was going to put it on. They had a lot of workers who used to keep a tab there and pay up at the end of every week, so they did not know they bought some drinks for the ladies.

Milt and I sometimes would be the last ones left when he was sorting things out to close. He had one client who would drink nothing but Crown Royal, which was expensive. What he used to do was fill the bottle up with the old cheap stuff, and nobody ever knew. While he was doing this, I was watching, and he would say "you'll not tell anybody about this will you". Anyway, one day this client went to a five-star restaurant down the road a bit, and ordered his Crown Royal. After he got his drink, he started fighting with the barman, saying he was not getting Crown Royal - he had been drinking that cheap stuff Milt was putting in the bottle for so long, that he did not know when he got the real stuff. He got into a fierce argument with the restaurant bartender. I was there when he came back and was telling Milt what had just happened. It was hard trying to keep a straight face.

Milt migrated out to California from either Chicago or New York back in the forties. He used to tell the story about the old car he came out in. His wife worked for a hotel company that had a hotel in Las Vegas. We made a few trips together out to Las Vegas. We would close the bar at about 4am, and drive out there and get there about 10 am. We would spend a couple of days there. Milt was a lot of fun to go to sporting events with, and we used to go to some baseball games out there also. Vince was very much into boxing and had a great film collection of old fight films which he used to show at the bar the one night a week he worked. I did see some great fights which I would otherwise never have seen. He had the film of the heavy-weight fight between Jack Dempsey and Gene Tunney, which your grandfather Pat went to see live at Municipal Stadium in South Philly. Jack Dempsey also made a visit over here to Carrigart, which is very much remembered over here.

All the while, the shop back in Pennsylvania was still doing excellent. My brother Eddie must have been having a hard time with my brother John waiting in the wings to take over. John was working in the Philadelphia Mint at the time, and with seven young kids he did not have too much extra cash at the end of the month. Eddie and himself cut a deal and he was in. That was the last place my brother Eddie worked, before he passed away with kidney problems. It was the first time John made that kind of money, plus he had some young lads who were able to help around the shop. He bought himself and the family a big house in Rose Tree, Pennsylvania, with the shop money which was nice. Meanwhile I was sinking fast in California. I never did have any problems with being humble, it happens to us all sometime. Keep your head up high and deal with it.

CHAPTER 2 - GOING BUSH

I do not remember exactly when I decided I was going to move on, which I do all the time anyway. Sometimes you win and sometimes you lose. The California project was a loss. Looking back now, I believe if I would have stayed and kept things going, I would have pulled it off. The truth is, we will never know. I started making a few trips down to Mexico and meeting some people. I came across a group who had purchased a sailboat, which ran into foul weather and ended up on thebeach in Cabo San Lucas, Mexico, which is the tip of the peninsula on the west coast directly south of San Diego. We dug it off the beach and got the engine going, and took it across the bay to the mainland, then had some sails made and fitted them on the boat. It was a forty-five-foot gaff-rigged ketch. It was built in Ecuador for a German gentleman who was taking it up to California, when he had problems off the coast of North Mexico, and ran it up on the beach. It was a very well-built sailboat with all wood and some very strong ribs.

Joe was still with me when I started winding things down. I found another job for the lad that came out from PA. I still had to sort Joe out. All the time he was out there he was never on a salary, as I used to just tell him if he needed money for anything just take it. Now that I was leaving on a sailboat heading toward South America, I had to sort him out. Before I left, I gave him 5,000 dollars to keep him going until he found something. One thing he asked me for was to give him the fish and chip shop. Again, looking back, I should have given it to him. The thing that I was concerned about was taxes and those people if they come down on you, they will nail you to the cross. I should not have feared them, but then again, his whole life from then on would have been different, so we will never know. He stayed out in California until the money was low, then he headed back east to mom and dad's place in the Villas. It was nice to have him there when they were getting up in years. I always believed that things always work out for the best. Next, the trip south.

South on a sailboat

This was another fun trip with some good boat-mates. It was my first trip on a boat and not a ship. The difference between a ship and a boat is, you can put a boat on a ship and not the other way around. There were five guys and one Canadian nurse, who was just tripping around like the rest of us. She was a real sport. It took us about three weeks to get the boat seaworthy and all the gear working. We could take on enough stores for about six days. The only navigational equipment we had was a compass. We did have charts for the Mexican coast. We had no refrigeration, so it was very hard to keep things for long. It was a slow trip, as nobody was in a hurry to get anywhere. If we found something on the chart that we thought would be fun, we pulled in and cleared customs. The papers we had were very suspect. The boat was registered in Ecuador and we were all Norte Americanos, and nobody could read Spanish. We had an Ecuadorian flag, but we did not know which side went up. I do not think any of the other port captains in Mexico knew either.

It was a pretty slow sailboat. It was very heavy, with not a lot of sail. It had a big belly and was a very strong and safe craft. The weather we hit all the way down was very fair weather, so we did not really have to see just how much of a beating the boat could take, but I felt it could take a good beating without breaking up. We stayed close to the coastline, as the coast of Mexico is pretty much of a straight line. We made several stops and stayed until we got things sorted with stores, and then we put the bow heading south again. We always kept a fishing line out and we usually had a big fish on there, which would be cooked up and eaten. We did eat a lot of fish. We would take one day's chicken and one day beef, but we could not keep it more than two days, so we ate fish. We always tried to bring as much fruit as we thought we could eat before it went off. It was a good diet without all the fat that we ate when ashore.

At a few ports we met up with some people who were heading south and if we thought we could get along and they would be fun to be around, we gave them a lift. At one time we had nine people on there, which was getting close. In fact it was too close, as we had an outbreak of hepatitis, which is a tough one to deal with in Mexico. There was also a lot of diarrhoea on there. As for me I did not get the runs or hep, so I was lucky there, for whatever reason. I still am a strong believer in a person's immune system.

Most of this happened when we were close to Acapulco. The engine also blew out on us when we were a couple of miles north of Acapulco. The winds were favorable, so we just sailed along. When we could see the lights of Acapulco, it seemed very close. There was a current down there and we were not making much headway for a long time. We decided to start the engine and motor, even though all the exhaust would be released into the cabin. We had sick people on there, and it was not comfortable. We were pretty much out of supplies too. We always kept some emergency fruit drinks stashed away for emergencies, which we so far had not had to use, so we all went up on deck and started the engine and motored into port. When we got to the dock, the boat was completely black with an inch or more of soot covering everything inside the cabin. All the same, we were glad to be in Acapulco, Mexico. We stayed the next three weeks in Acapulco, while we got the engine fixed and the cabin cleared up.

It was nice to take a three-week break from the boat. We still had a lot of Mexico to the south of us to sail. I and Dale, who had hepatitis and was a pretty sick pup, stayed at a motel, and I brought him all his food. I told the restaurant people he was sick, and to keep all his plates and utensils separate from the other guests. He decided to write poetry, which was some pretty morbid writing, but then again, in his condition and the way he was feeling, I can understand. He did hang tough in there and came through it. You could see the change after about two weeks. It started to turn around, and by week three he was back to his old self. I will write more about Dale later.

South from Acapulco

The three weeks went fast in Acapulco, and then off we sailed heading south along the Mexico coast. The second half of the Mexican coast was very sparsely populated, so there were not too many lights along the coast south of Acapulco. We pretty much went into every port to pick up supplies and the ports were pretty far apart. We were sailing along down there when we went a few days without hooking a fish, and we were down to rice and beans. We saw some small huts along the shoreline, and we decided to see if we could anchor outside the breakers and go ashore and see what we could pick up to eat. We went into our emergency ration cans of juice and put them in the dinghy and took them ashore with us. We managed to land, though it was a rough landing as the seas were big. We spent some time talking to locals who had some chickens running around. We made a deal to trade some juice for a chicken. Now for the trip back through the big waves to get back to the boat. We took a few waves into the dinghy, but made it through, if a bit wet.

We cooked the chicken that night and, as we were cooking the chicken, we saw some shrimp boats out there. We took the nurse who was on board in the dinghy, to see if we could get some shrimp from them. You always had to take a lady with you if you wanted some shrimp off them. They gave up a big bucket of shrimp and some ice to keep them fresh. So now we had chicken and shrimp. As we were enjoying the chicken, the fishing line went off and we had a big fish on there also. Things happen fast and all at once sometimes. We made it into a few more ports before crossing over into Guatemala.

It was good to get Mexico behind us. The main port on the Pacific coast of Guatemala, Puerto Quetzal, ships a lot of cotton out to the world. The big exports are bananas and cotton. After Mexico, the countries of Central America seemed very small, which they are. I think it took us a couple of days to get past Guatemala and into El Salvador. There are two main ports in El Salvador, the one I spent a bit of time in was Acajutla.

Hello, Bridget, Brendan and Maureen
El Salvador to Costa Rica

By the time we got to El Salvador, I felt like I had had enough of the sailboat, and it was agreed by all that I would leave the boat. Got my gear together and I was back onshore. I did not have much money, in fact, I only had forty dollars in Mexican money. I made arrangements to have some money sent to a Costa Rica bank which was about a thousand miles and three countries away. The sailboat had already sailed south for Panama and I was on my own in Acajutla.

I was staying in a room in a shop operated by an elderly lady who was very helpful – she took me in and secured my worldly goods. I decided I had more than I needed to carry, so I left some things there for her, as she had been very good to me. I stayed there for a few days, and she knew I had jumped ship and had no government stamps in my passport, if I even had a passport. She told me I should go down and see the Port Captain to get a stamp or some papers. So that is what I did, and I showed him my expired passport. I do not know if he even looked at the expiry date or not. What he did do was put a stamp in that read 'Port Captain, Acajutla, El Salvador' in my passport and I don't think he even signed or dated it.

I had met up with an American who was sleeping on the beach, who knew more about what was needed to cross land borders, as I had been on the sailboat from Mexico with different rules for seafarers. He told me we needed an exit visa from the government office in the capital of San Salvador. We hitch-hiked together up to San Salvador and talked to an immigration officer. He told me that an exit visa would cost me five bucks. I told him I had very limited funds and could he waive the fee. He got upset and told me that his countrymen, in order to travel to the USA, must have at least 1,000 dollars and I was down here with just forty dollars. I told him I understood completely and gave him the five bucks.

Now to figure out the land journey to Costa Rica. Myself and my newfound mate decided we would team up for the journey, and we started to hitch-hike. So out on the road we went. We had found out that the frontier between El Salvador and Honduras was closed, as they had had a big uprising at a football match between the two countries. In the history books it is known as the Football War.

Being that we could not travel through Honduras, we had to go to the southern tip of El Salvador and take a ferry across the bay to Nicaragua. It was a long way down to the ferry-port which was La Union. While we were hitching down the road we hooked up with a convoy of El Salvadoran trucks, about ten of them, all heading down to Costa Rica and Panama; we found a couple of drivers who said they would enjoy the company even though I did not speak much Spanish at all. My friend was traveling with one truck and I was in another. The trip to the ferry went well.

A real mind-blower was when we got on the ferry. I looked up on the bulkhead and saw a plaque that said 'built in Chester, PA'. Now Chester, PA was close to where I was raised, and I knew the shipyard very well. The ferry did look familiar, but I could not put it together at the time. They were the same ferries that the family used, to go down to the Jersey Shore where we had a summer home. So I travelled those ferries many times to cross the Delaware River. What happened was, they built a bridge from Chester to New Jersey, and they had to do something with those old ferries, and that is where they went to.

When we got to the other side of the bay and into Nicaragua, there was a shack there and some people came out and set up a table. That was the Nicaraguan immigration station. No problem getting a stamp. After that, it was a long trip on all dusty dirt roads full of potholes. We were on the road for five or six days and it was interesting the way they traveled in teams of two. What they would do is, the lead truck would pull over where he thought it would be a good place to get some shut eye. He had a hammock that he tied up under the truck and would sleep. I would just sleep on the ground; beggars cannot be choosers. It was hot, but I think I used to drink a gallon of water a day, and empty the bladder maybe at most once. A lot of sweat to cool the body temperature down.

Arrival in Costa Rica

It was nice to reach the frontier with Costa Rica. They kept us up there the whole day, as we had to unload and reload all the cargo for inspection. It gets awful hot hanging around the frontiers all day. I do not remember if we had any problems getting a visa to enter Costa Rica. I know that many people traveling that route had to buy a bus ticket out of Costa Rica in order to get in. I do not remember if they made us buy one.

I do know when we got to San Jose, the capital, I was down to less than a dollar. It was a Friday, and Monday was a holiday so that meant that I would not be able to check at the bank to see if my money arrived. Luckily, when I left California months ago, I had taken a camera with me that I had been hanging on to. I thought this would be a good time to let it go. I went into a camera shop which was run by a guy from Denmark or Belgium. I remember he offered me twenty-five bucks for the camera that I accepted with grace. He told me I could buy it back when my money came in. I never did buy it back. I had had it for months and never used it. Even to this day I am not good at taking pictures.

After the last month living off very little and traveling over a thousand miles, I felt very good with the money. I asked him where there was a cheap hotel, and he sent me to the Imperial Hotel. A very old house of three floors, all wood and a real fire trap, but cheap and clean. It was a great feeling to get between clean sheets and have a hot shower. Everything is about timing and to me it was better than a five-star hotel after the low-budget trip down there.

My beach-friend slept on the floor of the room. He was an amazing guy. During one of our conversations, for some reason Vietnam came up and he told me that he avoided the draft by being declared crazy. I had no problem with that. It got me thinking maybe I am the one who is crazy for getting involved, but I am still very proud to have been able to serve the country that I love with no regrets. Anyway, he got a hot shower and rinsed out some clothes. He was going on the road in the morning for Panama, which is a long trip.

The next morning, we had a full breakfast, and I gave him another five dollars for the final leg of his long trip. He asked me where he could send the money back to me when he got back on his feet. I gave him my sister's address. Must have been a few years later, she got a letter with five bucks in it and a short note. He was back in California; he had made it down as far as Argentina, where he was making surfboards and just about getting by. By then he was back in California doing the same thing, and he was back on his feet, with a few chips in his pocket. He was a great person who believed no debt is ever too small or too old to repay.

There were a lot of interesting people who stayed at the hotel. A lot of Peace Corps people stayed there, as it was clean and cheap. But now I was on my own again. Still thinking maybe I could make it down into South America and cross over to Africa. I heard the hardest part of the trip is south of Panama, where the road ends and there is nothing but bush. In the meantime, I was going to enjoy the capital city San Jose and all it has to offer. I found it to be a very cosmopolitan city with a lot of fine European restaurants. I really enjoyed my first stay there.

Panama trip

While staying at the Imperial hotel some of my mates from the sailboat also got a room there. It was great to see them and find just how the trip was from El Salvador to Costa Rica. Four of the crew had disembarked in Costa Rica before the sailboat departed for Panama.

While in San Jose someone purchased a car, and four of us decided to drive down to Panama. It was quite a trip, as there is a big high mountain you must get over. We crossed the Bridge of the Americas over the Canal. We then drove across Panama to the Caribbean city of Colon. From there we drove south to where the road stopped at the edge of the jungle.

The town was called Porto Bello if my memory is correct. They had a monument there with these big guns built, all facing out to the Atlantic. The story I heard was that an invasion was expected from the Atlantic, but as it turned out the invasion came from the rear and the guns were securely mounted facing the Atlantic and could not be turned around. When the landing for the invasion was made, all the ships' soldiers were very angry and wanted to go back. So, what the captain did was set fire to and scuttle the ships, so they could not return and the soldiers had no choice but to fight.

If anybody wants to travel south from there, they either have to find a boat or go on foot. Without the proper gear and knowledge, the jungle ahead is full of danger. In my head the plan was still to make it down as far as Brazil where the crossing from the south Atlantic Ocean to Africa is the closest. From there I thought I could find a way to make the crossing to Africa. Even though we made the trip back to San Jose, Costa Rica, and checked back into the Imperial hotel, I was still thinking and planning on moving on south. I found when you are traveling this way with limited funds, you are always crossing paths with other travelers coming and going in different directions, that always came up in the conversations. If they were coming from somewhere I was interested in, or they were going in the direction I just came from, we would always share information which was very helpful.

The trip back to San Jose was uneventful. We checked back into the Imperial hotel. We enjoyed San Jose, as it is pretty nice, with the many ethnic restaurants in the city. They also had some nice movie houses, with good recently released movies, which we found enjoyable as we were on the move for a long time and were now getting into what the city had to offer.

Cahuita - trip down

While there we got talking to some young Australian ladies who had just returned from the Caribbean side of Costa Rica. They told us about a settlement about 20 miles south of Limon, the main seaport for the export of bananas from the Caribbean coast of Costa Rica. They said they rented a house for a month and were told by officials that they had to leave after two weeks. They gave us directions to the house. It sounded like a fun trip. Here are the directions we were given. From the east side train station, take the train to Limon - it is about an eight-hour trip on a narrow gauge rail track. From Limon take another train to Pandora. After many stops you get off in Penshurst. From there you walk down to the river edge and get a dug-out canoe to cross the river. From the other side, you get a bus to Cahuita. That is where the house was with two weeks left on the rent. So, three of us made the trip. Dale from Michigan, Susie from California and myself.

It was quite a trip to find the place. The train was very rough, with wooden seats and a lot of twists and turns up over a high mountain. After the long train ride from San Jose, we passed a night in Limon, before getting the next train to Penshurst and on to Cahuita. The terrain from Limon to Penshurst was very flat with many stops. Once you got to La Bomba, that was the end of the road that ran along the track line. Going south from there the only access was by train, so anybody getting off the train carried supplies with them that were not available in the settlements.

Life in Costa Rica

Barney with David Leveaux and Rick Spencer in Cahuita

Boxing Event in Cahuita

Barney with friends, Richard and Van, and snook caught at Tortuguero

Barney with Rogelio in Cahuita

Van's brother, Don, a great entertainer and impersonator

There was access by dugout canoe from the sea if the settlement was on the sea, but most of the settlements had no access to the sea, so the train was the only way in or out. When you arrived in Penshurst and crossed the Estrella river, there were very few vehicles, no cars, only buses and trucks to get transport on the limited road system.

If you wanted to continue south and exit Costa Rica, that was possible. This is what you had to do - you had to travel by bus for hours with many stops, until you got to a place called Fields (the English name), or Bribri, which is the Indian name that is now used; that is where the road heading south ends. From there to the border with Panama, you take a very small gauge track train to the end of the line - a town called Bridgefoot which has a bridge over the Sixaola river, on which you walk over to Panama. They had well-armed guards on both sides, more so on the Panama side. When walking across there is a painted line that separates the two countries. Travel a bit more south and the road ends again, but they have a small air strip, where you can get a plane to Panama City. They also have a deep-water port to export bananas. So now you know the southern way out from what is known as the inside; most all travel out the same way they got inside.

Local people and local life

I found the people of Cahuita very friendly and helpful. They had few visitors due to the remoteness. Even in the seventies, 99 percent of people did not go anywhere on holiday if they could not drive there. No problem finding the empty house. So, it was nice to have two weeks free rent. The settlement was no way set up for major tourism. They had one hotel run by a Philippino. One general store run by a Syrian. Another shop run by a Chinaman and his family. They all spoke English, and a large percentage of the local population also spoke English as their first language, as most of the older blacks who migrated from Jamaica were English-speaking.

The Jamaicans had come over for the purpose of building a railroad for the banana company, to get the bananas to the port city of Limon for export. After the railroad became operational, they were given some land to grow bananas and a food garden. After they got that sorted, they would perhaps keep some animals. They formed their settlements anywhere along the coast that had a bit of a safe harbor. The settlements were about twenty miles apart as far south as Panama. The other two settlements south of Cahuita were Puerto Viejo and Manzanillo. Inland along the track line they could be closer.

There were big commercial farms like the one at the end of the railroad line, which is called Pandora, where the train makes a loop and heads back to Limon. The farm communities are numbered, which works. The difference is they are owned by the banana company.

One time I was down there with the Cahuita softball team to play a game with one of the farms. They all had a government official for investigations of things like accidents and such. There was an accident on the farm where two pickup trucks were involved. The official asked if I wanted to go for a ride, I said, yes. Got to the accident scene, and he wrote his report. There were no injuries thankfully, just some damage to the vehicles. I asked him, since the company owned both vehicles plus the road, and both drivers were employed by the same company what action would be taken? His reply was, perhaps one of the drivers would be terminated. A complete company owned community. A bit different from the system I was accustomed to living in.

It was a fun outing for the team and all the fans who made the bus and train trip. The train from Limon to Pandora was the only access into or out of the farms except for a small air strip. I would think today things are the same down there except for a road may have been pushed through that far, which may have opened the farms up a bit to easier access.

Back to Cahuita, which is not so easy to access but is fully open to the public. It is surrounded by privately owned cacao (chocolate) farms, the main crop that supports the community. Little did I know when I arrived in Cahuita that my travel plans would be put on hold for years. It only happened because of a conversation with two young Australian ladies about an empty house. I find it amazing that unknown strangers come into your life that can change the direction of your life.

Susie, Dale and I got settled into the unfinished two-story house on stilts, the ground level completely open with a stairwell going up to the second floor with two enclosed rooms and the rest open. The measurements were perhaps 20 by 30 feet. It had an outhouse. There was a rain barrel to collect water for drinking and other necessities. If you wanted to cook you had to make a fire with whatever was lying about.

They had three shops where you could buy groceries, though a very limited choice. The food was a bit more expensive, due to just how difficult it was to get supplies in. It's either by dugout canoe by sea from Limon, about a twenty-mile trip; or the train-canoe river crossing and transport to settlements inside. There was no electricity for the people of the settlement. There were three generators owned by the three shop owners. They only used them for a few hours during the day and a few hours in the evening. They were used mostly for the refrigeration and freezer units. Houses close to the hotel could purchase electricity from the hotel for a fee, based on how many lights bulbs they had.

Rice and beans were the mainstay in the diet. Fish was usually available when the sea was down, and the dugouts could get out to fish. There were few outboard motors for the canoes, and most of the fishermen used paddles to get out beyond the big breaking waves to troll for some fish. There was only one fisherman in the settlement who had a motor and a big enough canoe that could do the Limon return trip. As time went on, I got to know him very well as a friend.

As for meat, the farms around the settlement had cattle. The settlement had a butcher who would buy a beast off one of the farmers once a week and butcher it at first light. We would butcher it in the cocoa farm as there were trees that we could secure the beast to for the kill. That was Captain David's job. He done it very humanely. I won't go into how, but I had no problem with the way it was done. We would butcher the beast and quarter it and bury what was not edible. All the people who lived in and around the settlement would know, and if they had the money they would buy some fresh meat. Whatever meat was not sold on the day would have been salted to preserve it. Sometimes they would do a pig and it would be the same. That would happen more often when the cocoa crop was coming in, as there was more money around during that time. I got to know the butcher shop owner and butcher very well as time went on. More on that later also.

The canton of Talamanca

Talamanca is the least populated canton in Costa Rica. They had a saying that every child born had 60 hectares of land for him. Like a lot of places in the world, land is free in most of Talamanca if you can live there. When you get up in the inner area of Talamanca, there is a large reserve which is set aside for the Indians. The Indians do want to preserve their way of life from outside influences. The Indians are also the poorest of the Costa Rica population. If money and people came in from the outside, things would change. They get very few visitors in the reserve, other than non-government charities to help the people of the area. They do try and help them with freshwater solar power and help with agriculture and schools. Still this part of Costa Rica will continue to be the poorest.

I was once at a meeting when the topic came up and a lot of people thought it would be good to protect the Indian culture and most agreed with that. There was this very intelligent black man who did not, and he explained why. He said he spent all his working life trying to live in a multi-cultural society, and he could not vote to approve such a move. That was a pretty powerful statement. Anyhow, it was approved.

I was up there in the early seventies and I saw the place. I was up there again maybe twenty years later and there were little improvements, since no investments are being made other than non-governmental aid which is not much. People complain a lot about change, but what I say is when things stay the same and the people continue to fall behind the rest of the world, it is also not good. I will say it is one beautiful area of Costa Rica that few outsiders will ever get to see and experience. Any help for this area would be greatly appreciated.

I spent a long time in the area and did travel to all those inside places when I was based in Cahuita on the coast, about twenty miles south of Limon and about sixty miles north of the Panama border. Most of that travel involved fishing along the Caribbean coast, from Nicaragua to Panama, or traveling with a sports team. Throughout the area I became known as a sports promoter. Cahuita had a soccer (football) team, softball team and Domino team.

The borders are all very porous and the people were known more as coastal people rather than by the country where they lived; they usually had family on both sides of a border. I got to know the coastline very well, as well as all the river mouths, which change with time and weather conditions. To navigate them, you must know how to read them from outside the breakers coming in and inside the breakers going out. If the sea came up, it was good to know the closest safe harbor. There were no navigational aids along that part of the coast.

From the time I arrived in Cahuita I felt very welcome. The people I got to know were very knowledgeable about sports and world affairs. I noticed a lot of horses around the center of town. All my knowledge of horses was horse racing. So, I said to myself, let's have some fun and have a horse race. So I started talking horses and racing. I was told that years earlier they had horse races in the coconut walk along the white beach, but what happened was a rider was killed when his ride collided with a coconut tree. The sport was stopped. The community was still interested in doing it again. If a new location could be found, the community was open to it.

There was another long black beach on the north side of the settlement right in front of the baseball and soccer pitch, but there were a lot of big logs scattered all along the beach. To make it happen again, there was a lot of work to be done to make the beach fit for horse racing, as there was perhaps a mile of beach to be cleared of clutter.

The people of the settlement came out in force to clear the beach for horse racing. It took about a week to get the beach ready. The same people who had been the starter and the finish-line judge were still there, and they were only too happy to do it again. The horse owners came out of everywhere, and word spread up and down the coast and up in the hills. On the day of the races there was a big turnout. The whole of the school was there, as they had never seen anything like that before. We had a great turnout from other settlements along the coast, who came to enjoy a day in Cahuita. At the time, I had only been living in the settlement for about a month or two.

Visitors from outside

Dale and Susie were now heading back up to the USA. Since I got there a few more Americans had come into town from different parts of the States. Some rented houses and blended into the settlement, interacted with the local community and brought some new life into the settlement. A community within a community started to form. It was becoming popular through word of mouth. It was an interesting place to lay back and just enjoy your surroundings.

It was pretty much subsistence-living for the locals. All that you had really, was the sea for fish, lobster and turtle. The land was used for crops, the main cash crop being cocoa. To a lesser extent plantain, coconut and a lot of fruit trees. Because of our distance from the market and the logistics, most of the fruit went right back into the ground. The planting of all the fruit trees was still great planning by the original settlers, who also had gardens with a lot of root vegetables, pineapples and other things. It was a limited choice of food but all healthy food. Trash was not a problem as there was very little of it. For the most part, poor people do not pollute. Looking at the world today with all the plastic particles in every animal or fish, I can appreciate the place more now for the things we did not have.

As new people arrive, they bring in new things. Surfers showed up with their surf-boards. The locals grew up around the sea and the waves all their lives. These surf-boards got their interest. A new sport was introduced to them. It took off, and today surfing is so big in the area for the good reef breaks when the sea is up. Surfers will travel far off the beaten track looking for a good wave to ride. No place is too far or too hard to get to - if they know a good wave is there, they will go. What surfers do not like is a lot of other surfers looking for a few good waves.

There was also some baseball equipment kept in a house next to the field. It was not much stuff but enough to get a pickup game going. With new visitors arriving, I would always ask them if they played any baseball, and would they like to take part in a pickup game. It was a great way to blend in to the settlement and meet new people.

From talking to the older men of the settlement, I found out where a lot of their knowledge of American sports came from. They had a very strong connection to Panama, where they went to work during the Second World War and Korean War. Most of the workers went to Colon, Panama which is on the Caribbean side of the canal and much smaller than the Panama City side. When the work dried up, they came back up to Limon and the smaller settlements along the coast. For most of the black community, English was their first language, Spanish their second. In Cahuita they had two school systems, one English, one Spanish. The English school was eventually closed, but the black population continued to speak English at home, so the children also spoke English, but for the most part they could not read or write English. In the Spanish school they could learn to read and write Spanish, so as time passed, Spanish was understood by more people. When I was there the older black people only spoke English. When a Spanish-speaking person tried to talk, they sent them to a younger person who understood Spanish. Now all the local people speak Spanish which is the way it evolved.

Growth of tourism

When I arrived down there in Talamanca in the early seventies, cocoa was the cash crop. It wasn't always like that. The area was originally planted out with bananas. The bananas took sick with a disease that came up through Panama and so was called the Panama sickness, which destroyed the entire crop. That is when cocoa was introduced to the area and it thrived. The price was much more flexible than the bananas, some years were great and some not so great, like any type of farming. One year was so good they were joking about buying gold teeth for their horses and mules.

There were always plenty of bananas and plantain around to eat, and a market outside if you could get enough to make it worthwhile. There were also a lot of nice large hardwood trees available, but difficult to get out, like everything else. There was talk about building a road and bridges over the three rivers, so you could drive right up to Limon which would open the area up to the outside. They also had plans for bringing in some large generators for all the houses in the center of the settlement. This was all in the hope of getting outside investment in tourism. What was also happening at this time was the cocoa was being taken over with an airborne sickness that was destroying the whole crop.

So, the area was going through a big change, and when they lost the agriculture base, they decided to move into tourism. That was quite a transformation. It was what I was doing for a couple of years until I got a bit burned out, and they started doing the same thing with slightly better accommodations, perhaps one star at the most. The local community all got involved. Small visitors' accommodations were being built all along the beaches and in the settlement by the ones who previously had cocoa farms. What was in the air during this time was a National park on the south side of the settlement, which included the fishing camps area. The interest in the area was increasing daily from outside the zone with new investors trying to cash in on the tourist trade.

Visitors to Barney's place

I became part of that in a small way. The house I was renting for ten dollars a month was more room than I needed. So, when some people found the place and got off the bus in the center of the settlement, they would ask where they could stay, and the locals would bring them up to me. A few of them would even ask for where my place was, as mine was the only place they could stay and smoke all the pot they wanted. They would ask how much to stay, and I would say 25 cents a night. There was a book going around called how to live on five dollars a day. Even back in the seventies that was very cheap.

As new people arrive, they bring in new things. A doctor and two friends arrived and they rented a house owned by the woman who had the hotel, it was a nice place right on the sea. So we started to chat, and I asked if they played poker, as I was pretty knowledgeable on all edicts involved in a good poker game. So, sure enough, we got a poker game going at Doctor David's rented house. We had six players, Doctor David and his pet pizote (also known as a coatimundi), who went everywhere with him. Doctor David now has his own house and a cocoa farm down there. There were also John J., Francis, and two surfers (Bill and Billy) who were very popular with the locals, who had never seen a surf board that somebody could actually stand up on. And myself.

We then sorted out the betting limit and the different poker games we were going to play. I like to limit it to three games: seven-card stud, five-card stud and draw poker. The game started about midday. It was a fun game with good poker players. Poker is a great game to get to know people - we played all through the night, which was great fun, and we all knew each other much better.

I always had a good flow of guests coming through. Some very interesting people doing interesting things. I will tell you about a few of them. I had people come looking for me from as far away as central Mexico. It was all word of mouth.

One time I had three young lads in their late teens or early 20s, from Long Island, New York, probably from well-off families. They did not talk much about themselves, but one story they told me I thought was funny. While in high school the principal found some pot in their school locker or in their pockets. With them being young and with the stigma of pot at that time in white society in America, they were scared when the principal had them in his office. They asked the principal not to tell their mother. I guess they were more scared of their mom than the police or they thought the principal would not bring the police into it. They had a small allowance to live on, and they found they could live down in the bush and smoke all the grass they wanted, as it was cheap and without fear. I do not think they ever left the settlement other than Limon for the entire stay. They stayed for a few months and then went back to New York. Then about a year later they came back, when I had the house that I bought a bit outside the settlement, close to the ballpark. For a while there, it was just me and them there. When the place got a bit untidy, I would say the government may be around today. They would clear the place of pot seeds and hide their stash out in the yard. The government never came but that made no difference. They were well-behaved young lads who enjoyed smoking pot, to put it mildly.

This is the generation that brought about the changes in the law pertaining to marijuana that we are seeing all over the United States today. Prior to this time, marijuana was always available in the black neighborhoods. The government did not get involved so long as it stayed there; but, during the time when the civil rights movement took hold, the white population was turned on to pot and that was a no no. The government came down hard on anyone who ever came in contact with it. I knew one fellow in California who spent five years in jail for having one joint. The white people with power in the justice system were scared to death of the 'deadly weed' and were determined to put an end to it in their community with long, long jail terms. That is why the three lads from Long Island, New York found so much comfort living down in the bush. They are also the ones who went back home and got active in changing the law, to make it legal for medical and recreational purposes. These freedoms that the populace now have are still very new and evolving. Since then they have found a lot of medical uses for the herb, and I believe they will find more, as it is open now to research where before it was not.

Another great guest I had was from the University of Toledo who was down there collecting bugs - we did have plenty of them. He had all his bush gear. Every morning he would get his net and little bottles and gas that he would euthanize them with. He would be off, and I would not see him until late afternoon, when he would sort out his day's catch and pack it away. We would talk about bugs and his studies. I asked him if he found a bug that had not been discovered yet, how would they name that bug. He told me he would be allowed to name the bug. He told me he would name the bug after me. If you ever hear of a barney bug, you know where it came from! He was up at first light and off with his big bug net. A lot of the bugs down there come out at night, but I do not remember him bug-hunting at night. The people of the settlement really liked him and loved to chat with him about all the bugs he was collecting to take back to Canada. They helped him with the local names of the bugs, as they also were very tuned into the environment that he was researching.

There were a few 'good ole boys' from central Florida who were great sports people, mostly hunting, fishing and surfing. They adapted easily to life in the bush, as they were well used to camping and tuning into the environment for the wealth and beauty of it. Those boys had their act together. One fellow started to build fiberglass fishing boats. He shipped down a speed boat from Florida, and made a mold for making new ones. Up until now all the lobster fisherman used big heavy dugout canoes, this was a big change from the canoes that were used by all the fishermen.

They also had some good fishing gear that some local fishermen refused to use. The locals used nothing but heavy gauge fishing line wrapped around an old bottle. It was amazing how much fish they caught considering the gear they used. Sports fishing was something alien to them.

I had this other group of four from Argentina who were traveling up to Canada. The way they were traveling was, they all had skills working with leather. So, what they would do was find a place like I had, which had a bit of security. They would buy enough leather to make maybe a hundred ladies' handbags. When they ran out of leather, they would take their bags up to the capital. They worked away for about a month and loaded up their bags and headed up to San Jose to cash in their bags. From there, they would head up to the next country, and I would think do the same thing again. They were very nice hard-working lads. They left me a couple of bags which I took back up to the States and gave one to my sister, and I forget who got the other one. My sister loved it as they were good quality bags.

Brother Joe's visit

There was a constant flow of travelers who stayed a short time and then moved on in different directions. The most important visitor I had was my oldest brother, Joe. This was after Eddie, my next to oldest brother, passed away, and I was not aware of his death until three weeks later, when I got a letter from my sister who passed the news on to me. My brother, Joe, at the time was staying with my sister. I went up as far as Limon to make a phone call home to talk to them. The whole family took it hard as it was unexpected for us. He was on a kidney machine once a week, but my brother had offered one of his kidneys and he was just waiting for it to happen.

My brother was not there, but I asked my sister if he could come down to see me, and to give him some money for the trip. He was not too busy at the time, so he had the time. He said he would make the trip and I was a bit surprised, as he never did travel much. When my sister gave him the directions, he thought it was a joke. Plane, train, another train, walk down to the river, get in a dugout canoe to cross the river, and get a bus to Cahuita. When he got to Limon, the train was a few hours late and he felt himself getting a bit upset. He looked around as there was a lot of people waiting for the same train and he was the only one getting even a bit upset. So, he accepted it as being a normal occurrence.

While on the train to Penshurst he was talking to another norteamericano who said he was going to Cahuita also. They were talking away and the young lad was looking for my place also. The traveler's grapevine. He landed in Cahuita on the last bus of the day. I was in the pub across the road from where the buses discharge passengers. A good friend came over across the road and told me my brother was there. Most all the people who travel too hard to get places carry backpacks; my brother was not one of them. I went to see him, and he was sitting on a bar stool having a beer, with his suitcase next to him.

I still remember my first words: Well, we lost a good man. He told me the story of how things went down with the viewing, and how his wife and our mother were taking it. He did say my mother took it very hard, as it was the first child she lost. She kept saying she wishes it was her and not him. Eddie was a very easy-going person who was liked by all. He had also served a tour of duty with the Army in Korea during the war.

Joe stayed maybe about four weeks. He had a very enjoyable time, talking and just enjoying the people. One story he liked to tell was when I had two other young Americans staying there with me when he was there. They had a real nice dog traveling with them that they left there. Anyhow, they wanted to climb up a coconut tree to get some coconuts. They had ropes and they were trying all day. I had a good friend of mine cutting and clearing up the yard. He and my brother were watching all this going down. Late in the day, Alfonzo, my worker, had to help them out. So, he went over, put his arms around the coconut tree, walked right up to the coconuts and cut a few for the lads, who were standing at the bottom with their jaws wide open in amazement.

<u>The horse v. the mule</u>

Another bit of fun that Joe loved was the horse/mule race. Our local character, Waggie, had a mule that he thought a lot of, that was known as Moon Mule. We were talking one day, and he told me how fast his mule could run. Now we know mules can't run fast but he kept up with it. He told me his Moon Mule could beat my horse in a race. I really did not think a mule could run faster than my horse, even though my horse was not a fast runner. So we decided to have a race for some fun, as the black beach was all cleared for racing now. Anytime you are having a race, it draws attention, even if it's only turtles. It did draw a lot of attention. I knew my horse Goma was not in great shape, but I still thought she could beat a mule. Waggie did work this mule a lot, so he knew him well - so the race was on. It was a fair race and guess who won? Waggie's famous Moon Mule won by half a length. The race was enjoyed by all who attended, so it was a great day in the settlement.

So Joe went back home with a lot of stories. My sister said when he got back, she had never seen him talk so much. In turn it really got her interested in the place, and she did get down there years later for a visit.

Visit from my nephew, Chuck

Someone else from my family who got to know Cahuita was my young nephew, Chuck, my sister's older son. After I had been down in Cahuita for a year or so, I took a trip back to the US to see them. When I came back down, I brought Chuck, who was 10 years old, for a 2-week visit. It was his first trip on an airplane, and he was amazed to be served food on the flight. He was very marked by that visit, and later, when he was working for Verizon, he formed a non-profit company (contributing $30,000 of his own money), and spent six years down in the Talamanca region, helping to build up computer skills in the local schools, establishing computer labs for developing applications, networks and repair in over 40 schools, training technicians to build and repair computers. For this, he and his company shipped in around 1000 computers over five years. His inspiration for this was his original experience in Cahuita at 10 years old, and his later observation of the contrast between wealthy and poor communities in the US, where deprived schools suffered from a lack of computers to develop essential technology skills among children - otherwise known as the digital divide.

Baby's death and funeral

While I was living down in Cahuita, something very sad happened - I had a local girl friend who had a five-year-old daughter she was raising, and she and I also had a daughter of our own, who only lived for 27 days. She went up to Limon to give birth and brought the baby right back. It was about midday and there were a few of us around, when she came screaming out of the room saying 'my baby is dead'. It was a very sad day, we tried to comfort her as well as we could. There was no doctor in the settlement, so what happened is the local government representative, who is known as the judge, made a report of what happened. Nobody really knows what happened other than that it was a crib death.

The law of the bush is the body must be buried before sundown the next day. The people in the settlement are well used to death. Daniel, a local builder, made a small coffin and lined it with white linen. The body was laid out all night with people paying their respects, some saying prayers. The next morning, she was taken to the cemetery where a grave was prepared for her and she was put to rest. What I had to pay for was the making of the coffin with white linen and preparing the grave, which cost a total of about eight dollars. It was two days forever etched in my mind. After that, me and her mother drifted apart and we lost contact. The next part of the death rituals was what was known as 'nine night' when the soul rises to heaven. This was a tradition that came with the Jamaican settlers, a nine-day wake, with lots of rum and local food.

I remember another funeral of a very respected local man, Solomon, who used to have a place down on the white beach. He had moved up to the settlement, very sick and had been there for days. I stopped by to see him, he was clearly in bad shape and needed more help than was available where he was. I talked to Carlos Tobash, a shop owner who had transport, I told him how bad I thought Solomon was and asked if he could get him up to the hospital in Limon hospital. Carlos' brother Jose went over to see Solomon and he took him in his vehicle to Penshurst and crossed the river; but while he was walking up to the train station, he collapsed and passed away. They brought his body back to the settlement and prepared him for a viewing. It was a long night with lots of guaro. Miguel was there, he and Salomon were very good friends from the fish camp, where Miguel stayed for a short period, as he did have a family up in Limon. Solomon was layed to rest in the local graveyard.

During this period there were several deaths in the settlement and surrounding area. There were some people I knew during this period that decided to leave the area and spend some time up in the capital San Jose. I suspect it was because of dengue fever as it is prevalent in the area. The term the locals used was the gripes, and without any medical analysis, we will never know for sure.

Visitor or resident?

As time went on, I was spending a lot more time with the locals and with the long-term visitors. When new people showed up, I would invite them to play in a softball game or soccer game. I was more like a resident of the settlement than a visitor. As time went on, some of the long-term visitors started applying for residents' cards, which involved a lot of paperwork with government officials and lawyers. As for me, I would just let my visa run out and wait until I wanted to go home or exit the country other than through Panama or Nicaragua, where there was no immigration official at the border. If there was one there, I would just say I had no papers on me and it was a short stay. Then when I had to fly through a major airport where they would look for an exit visa, I would get to immigration and tell them I overstayed my visa and pay a small fine and get the visa. I found that the easy way for me to deal with immigration. That all changed after the disaster of 9/11/2001.

Trip to the interior

One time I went off on my own to explore the rough inside trail up through Bribri and west along the Sixaola River. The road that went up along the Sixaola river was built by the banana company. The road going up along the Sixaola river does not get much traffic. The banana farms along the road were wiped out by the sickness that came up from Panama.

When I made the trip up, I got a horse in Fields from an old black man who was known as Daddy. I had never spent much time around horses. Off I went, me and the horse and a small bag with some food, blanket and some rain gear. The horse really did not want to make this trip. On the way up, there were a few small creeks that we had to cross. Every creek we got to, the horse would stop and drink water and want to turn around and go back. I had to really coax him to continue.

We went through one place with a few houses, called Chase, but I did not see any people. One house had a sign in English that read 'we buy dollars'. I could see the other side of the river, which is Panama, so perhaps there were some travelers who had dollars to sell. I kept on going for hours, till I came to a place called Bamboo which does not show up on any maps. There was a shop there and a fellow who owned it by the name of Lewis. I am sure he did not get many visitors who came up from Fields walking alongside a horse because the saddle came loose. I was not quite capable of getting it back tight enough to mount the horse. I talked to Lewis who spoke English, he had a woman and some young children. His business was mostly with Indians and a few others who came to clear land. A fellow from Nicaragua was also there, and spent the night like me in a small little one-room wooden structure on stilts, a short distance from the small shop and house.

I later heard that the Nica who I talked to had to leave. He spent a lot of time building fences to keep cattle. He had mostly Indian neighbors who all kept their own pig. Well, what happened was the Nica had his little wooden house and garden. While he was gone, a pig got into his garden more than once and did a lot of damage to his garden, which he depended on for food. He ended up killing the pig. This caused a serious problem with the neighbors. From what I heard, every time he went to the farm he was making, he found one of his cattle killed. He had no choice but to leave. A year or two later, I did hear he was back up there and got the problem sorted, how I do not know. I would think he had to pay somebody for the pig he killed.

The trip back down to Fields was no trouble as the horse was very happy to be going home, and only stopped at a very few creeks to sip some water and continue at a good pace. Much faster pace than the trip up.

Trip north through the canal

My first trip up the canal was with an American living down in Cahuita who was known as Cockeye, because he had one eye looking crosswise from an accident as a kid. When his mother came down for a visit, he decided he wanted to take her on a trip up the canal. Miguel and his mate, Cheapie, are well known fishermen, with a big dugout and a 25 horsepower motor that they made available to take people up the canal.

The first time I got to know Miguel was when he came down the fish camp to stay for a few days, while he was waiting to pick up some herb from one of his growers to take up to Limon, where he had a good market. While we were there at the fish camp another big dugout came in; it was a high-level Limon official who wanted to talk to Miguel, who said he had also wanted to talk to him for a long time. They did have their talk, and then a group of us went into what they called the bluff, which was the center of the settlement with the pubs. It was about a two mile walk along the edge of the white beach – the same beach which is now a National Park and there are no more fish camps. The last camp down there was Captain David, who was the butcher that I worked with in the butcher shop. The official stayed the night down at the camp and left out the next morning.

As time went on, I got to know Miguel well and found him to be of good character. For the trip north up the canal, we loaded the dugout (Santa Rosa) in Limon with a 55-gallon barrel of gasoline and some supplies, and headed north with Miguel at the helm. A short sea voyage around Limon port to Moin, where we entered the canal to head north.

When you first head up the canal you are greeted with dense jungle, with all kinds of birds and sounds. There is not much traffic on the canal, and it is not very wide maybe twenty-thirty feet. The waters are still, with some shallow places where you must slow down. The next river mouth from Moin is Matina; we went past the river mouth and continued up the canal to Parismina. There they had a real nice sports fish camp which had a good custom, as it was expensive - 150.00 dollars a day all inclusive. We went into the camp and they offered up a fine meal. It was run by two sisters whose father started the camp and passed it on to them.

Miguel found a friend he knew from Puerto Viejo who knew of an empty camp. The camp was on the north side of the river mouth. The camp was about a half mile up the beach from where we left the dugout and motor with someone who was living in a camp on the north side of the river mouth. The camp that we were told about was built there to grow some corn and harvest, but the camp was then abandoned to the rats. When we got there the place was infested with rats and it was night, so we had to stay. You just must stay the night and throw something over your head and try and get some sleep and let the rats have the run of the place.

    At first light the next morning we were up and ready to go. We made a fire and got some coffee and some johnnie cake - which is just dough fried in some coconut oil and eaten. We headed back to the boat and motor, and there was a real nice lagoon there. We stayed there for a few hours and bathed and washed the clothes we were wearing the night before. It did not take long for them to dry in the hot sun. The owner of the house brought us out some rice and beans and fresh fish, so we also had a good meal while waiting and just enjoying the pretty much untouched environment. That was as far north that we got on that trip. The trip back down to Limon was pretty much uneventful. We did see some small tow boats, towing a lot of logs out of the jungle to the sawmills of Costa Rica.

    My friend's mother was concerned about him living where he was and wanted to check it out herself. I know she enjoyed the trip and found it rough but interesting, but was also glad to get back to better accommodations. I also found the trip a bit rough but still enjoyable, and knew I would want to make more trips to explore the canal right up to the border. Prior to this trip most of my travels had been along the southern coast of Costa Rica. My friend and his mother went up to San Jose, to see his mother off for the States. I found my way back to Cahuita, and got back into what was happening in the settlement.

Other river trips towards Tortuguero

    At some point, I started fishing and camping with the good ole boys and exploring the northern coast. The north side of Limon to the Nicaragua border was quite different from the south side down as far as

Panama. The first little fishing village a few miles north of Limon is Portete, where lobster was big when it was happening. The next little village is Moin. This is where the road ends and there is a railroad bridge over the canal going out to the sea that you can walk across. The railroad is for travel inland to towns and villages only accessible by rail.

To travel north along the coast, they have man-made canals connecting the rivers coming down from the mountains to the coast. These canals were built by the US Army Corps of Engineers many years ago. You can travel them all the way up to Nicaragua without having to navigate the sea. They have a public service barge that leaves Moin every day. For the people who live along the canals and rivers and do not have their own transport, this is their only service. It's a very slow-moving barge that makes many stops. It takes over 24 hours to make the trip up to the Barra del Colorado on a barge that leaves Moin daily.

Along this waterway there are some tourist fishing camps for sports fishermen and woman. They are a welcome cash flow for the local fishermen, who are employed as guides for the guests. These camps are first class and very expensive. The main sports fish that they are looking for is tarpon which can weigh up to a 150 pounds and can fight. It is a catch and release fish. Because of their bony mouths, they usually throw the hook out themselves with a big jump out of the water. The other fish that is enjoyed by those who fish for food or for sport is big snook. It is some great sports fishing that me and the Florida boys had the good fortune to do a lot of. We had a safe house down in Cahuita where we kept our fishing gear and boats and motors. We also had plenty of camping gear.

We made several trips up to Tortuguero which is maybe an hour or more of a boat trip up to Barra Del Colorado and the Nicaraguan border. We had a nice camp site in Tortuguero where we could camp, and there was a local fisherman and his wife lived on the same land right on the river. It was a great set-up, where the fisherman's wife, whose name was Marta, was a refugee from the war going on in Nicaragua between Somoza and the Sandinistas.

On one trip up there, it was just me and Billy (the same Billy from the poker game). Marta had one daughter about five and was pregnant with another. Every morning when we woke up, Billy had to go back to see Marta, and she would have coffee ready for us. So one morning Billy went back to see Marta for our coffee, and he came back to me and said 'this will blow your mind'. I said what is it, and he said Marta had a baby boy last night, while we were sleeping maybe twenty yards away on the river bank, and we did not even know. She still had our coffee ready in the morning - she was one strong lady. Marta named the baby Barney, which I suppose was an honor!

Maybe a hundred yards up the river, close by the river mouth, there was a first-class fishing lodge that had their own airstrip to bring in the fishermen and women. The owner was a young wealthy German fellow who loved fishing. It was a beautiful camp that catered to fishermen and bird watchers. We would stop up to see him and got to know him pretty well. He would let us use his freezer to keep the fish we caught. He also kept five or more nice parrots that made a lot of noise. There was one fellow who had a beautiful chicken-hawk that he kept and trained and took good care of. For some reason, he had to make a trip out and he asked the owner if he could leave his bird at the fishing lodge, as he knew there were other birds there. He left instructions on what to feed him and how much. His weight was checked everyday before it was feeding time, as was his feed. This went on for a few days, he would fly off and fly around and then come back. I think it was about the third day when he left his perch and he flew right across the garden to where the noisy parrots had their perches and flew down and grabbed one of them, and flew off and never came back. Those parrots and all that squawking for days was just too much for the hawk to cope with.

Trip south along the coast

There was another fun trip that I made later, with a mate who had made a trip up through the canals as far as Parismina with his mother. This time we headed south along the coast to well past where the road ended, a short distance south of Puerto Viejo. At the time I had two horses that did not get much work. One was a nice pony of about six years and very mellow. The other was a young filly that had just turned two. So, me and my friend, Cockeye, we got the horses ready one morning and headed off south along the beach, down past the fish camps and around the point (where rumor has it a treasure is buried). We made it around to Vargas, where there were a few more camps. One was the camp of a future judge in Cahuita. That is another story for later. We passed them and headed on down the beach to Hone Creek, which is a pretty big creek to cross when heavy rains come. The water was not so high, so we had little problems crossing, as it was only about chest high and not a heavy flow.

That day we made it down as far as Puerto Viejo. We stayed at a friend's house down there as we knew the trail was only going to get more difficult as we went south from Puerto Viejo. The road ends not far south of there, with a trail for horses and foot travelers, as there are still small camp sites along there and a few creeks to cross.

The next settlement along the coast is Manzanillo which at that was only accessible by dugout canoe, walking or horseback. It was a pretty small settlement, with one big family by the name of Maxwell, who owned the one shop and pub. There were several other families that lived down there, doing their fishing and farming. We camped out a short distance from Manzanillo. The mosquitoes were really bad, so what we did was collect some green bush and dry scrub and lit a fire at the top of the beach on the sea side of the hump and let the breeze from the sea take the smoke over top of us, so we could get some sleep and keep those blood-sucking bugs at bay. The next day we were in Manzanillo.

It was my first time down that far south along the coast. The great family that owned the shop was Maxwell, a man who was well known all along the coast. We then left Manzanillo and headed south past Monkey Point. We found a trail and it was a very steep grade up and down. There were places where we had to dismount and lead the horses as there was no way you could stay in the saddle. The trail was very narrow, and we went by a camp where a fisherman was living, who told us he was washed out by the rising sea twice when he had his camp on the beach, so he moved his camp where that would never happen again, at least not in his lifetime. (That is climate change). While we were talking, we found out we had a great friend in common with Miguel, or Mouth as he was known. That was the same gentlemen who made the trip up north to Parismina with me.

All along the trail there were no other animals visible. We made it down as far as Monkey Point Lagoon as it was called. I knew a friend there who sometimes traveled through Cahuita, where he would pass a night on his way up to Limon and back. His name was Germán, he had a nice camp down there with his wife who kept chickens and grew vegetables. There were two other camps down there, one occupied by a Mr. Brown, and I do not know who had the other. What I do know is that you could look down the beach as far as the eye could see, and see nothing but beautiful beach.

It was also the closest place where you could depart for Boca Del Torres Island which belongs to Panama. It is the best and easiest to access from coming around the Monkey Point Keys and into the safe lagoon, and getting out was just as easy. The last time I was in there on a dugout canoe with Miguel and Cheapie, we had some turtle and we butchered them there, and there were a few dogs hanging about. We would clean the bones of meat and throw the bones out in the lagoon and the dogs would swim out and dive to get the bones.

This time it was by horse and we spent a couple of days talking to German. When we were there a Spanish man showed up on horseback with a horse and a small pack. The horse was very dirty with mud from his trip down from Manzanillo. He sold his horse and saddle to German cheap. The last I saw of him was his back walking towards Panama. I asked German if he thought he stole the horse and saddle, and he said yes, but he would let word get back to Manzanillo and the owner would buy it back off him.

What German also told us was that nobody ever took horses up over the trail we came on. That trail we took was just for foot traffic. All animal traffic went around the three big hills from Manzanillo to Monkey Point. So, when we headed back north, German put us on the trail. We left early and it was a difficult trail to follow as it was very muddy, and we kept just looking to see other horse hoof marks in the mud. We could not dismount with the mud, and the thought was always there that the horses could belly out where they would sink up to their bellies and could not get out. That did not happen, but when we did stop to look where we thought the trail was, we and the horses would be covered with mosquitoes. We kept on going just hoping that we were still on the trail, and would soon hear the sea breaking on the beach. There was no way I could think of that we could have survived the night in that mosquito-infested swamp. It was late afternoon when we did hear the sea breaking on the beach and it was the most beautiful sweet sound. We passed the night at Maxie's pub, before heading back to Puerto Viejo.

Cahuita's judges

Now back to the fish camps and the future judge. The one camp belonged to Alejandro who had been camped down there for a while. We had a chat with him, and he said we would see him soon be in Cahuita. Here is the story I heard - he came into Cahuita while the judge who had the job was up in Limon, and he just went in and took over the job, and so the government had no problem.

He made a trip up to Limon and went into the commander's office and was told to turn in the big .45 caliber gun he carried tucked in his belt. What he told the commander was, when he takes out his pistol he will be shooting it. So, he was the new judge for Cahuita. He had more weapons that he kept in his government office in Cahuita.

I remember on New Year's day, me and another well-known lad from a large family in the settlement were walking by and were called over. He brought out an automatic AR-15, showed it to us and then we all started firing rounds off. He wanted everyone to know what he had. He also had to have a deputy and he found a good one that was well-known in the zone.

Alejandro was extremely interested in the drug trade and he wanted to be part of it. One of my chance sellers (more about my chance bank later) was also known to supply pot to people. He had always been incredibly careful to keep the judge out of his business. Well, Alejandro called him into his office and gave him a bag of weed, and told him he had to sell it for him. So, he was now also working for the new judge.

He was a remarkably interesting judge. He had some pictures of him with Fidel Castro, as he had spent some time in Cuba. He was a full-on Commie. The powers-that-be in the settlement were watching him to see what kinds of moves he was going to make. They really did not care about the pot sales as there were more important things that could go bad.

The Costa Rica government had a limit on how much the food staples could be sold for. Well, that was all well and good if you lived in the capital, where things are awfully close. When you are living down in the bush, the cost goes up due to the hardships of getting supplies in there. Well, he found a shop that was selling rice above the government price limit. So, him being a good commie, he confiscated all the rice in the shop and gave it free to the poorer people of the settlement. That ruffled some feathers in the settlement, and it was not long before he was on the list of past judges.

The next judge that we got came from north of Limon, and he was there for a while. His weakness was he was into thieving. With more and more visitors coming in all the time, there were more and more easy marks for the thieves. It was interesting when a tourist had something stolen and they would report it to him. The judge would take down all the facts and tell the victim that he would investigate. The only time he would investigate was when he did not get his piece of the action. The settlement knew there was a good future in the tourist trade, and having tourists being robbed was not good for tourism. He was also soon gone, and on the list of past judges.

There were some settlements that had no judge for a good reason. Judges have been known to get killed if they pushed the envelope too far. If that happened more than once, then nobody would take the job. I really think that higher up in the security forces, they liked having these settlements where nobody wanted to be a judge. What would happen is, if they had a judge who they for some reason wanted out of the security forces, they would assign them to one of these settlements, and they would have to resign from the force. That happened to one judge I knew very well, and he got a good job in security working with a good American company and being paid more money with less perks.

Since the tourist industry really exploded, they have much more security. The last time I was down there they had around 10 guards plus the judge. I had a good talk with a well-informed friend about the security situation. What happened was, some of the new guards were

Costa Ricans from first generation Nicaragua parents. A lot of Nicaragua refugees arrived from the Somoza-Sandinista war in the early to late seventies. There were some people in the settlement who were not yet ready to accept Nicas in the security forces, but for the most part, the people of the settlement accepted them as though they were Ticos (Costa Ricans).

Drug tourism

All the north Americans that did come down for a visit, I believe was because of the easy availability of marijuana for sale. The availability of the weed did produce a bit of drug tourism which was welcomed and accepted by a very large proportion of the settlement. It has been available in the area since the Jamaicans introduced it when the railroad was being built. This is the seventies when it was picking up popularity in the USA, and the punishment for having and smoking marijuana was very severe, to put it mildly.

There was a small amount of drug tourism happening along the Caribbean coast. At that time there was no access to harder drugs that I knew of. It was later that crack cocaine showed up in bulk and all the problems associated with it came into play. The Cahuita community, which had a high tolerance for drugs, dealt with the problem rather well. Marijuana was never a problem as far as anti-social behavior was concerned. I, like most all the foreign visitors who settled into the life in the settlements, was fond of the herb. Coming from where I was coming from, the government destroyed more lives with the enforcement of the laws than the herb itself could ever cause. If everyone had accepted the law, then it would never have changed.

As for me personally, I did not pay the marijuana law no mind. At the same time, I was not in-your-face smoking the herb. When I made that decision, I became an outlaw but never considered myself a criminal. There was a herb network that I became involved in. The business was the same as all business supply and demand. I became a fringe player on the supply side of the business, and not because of the money. I believed it was a good drug, and should be made available for public consumption. I became very suspicious of anything the government said or published about the drug. This was not easy for me, like for many others, who would like very much to believe that their government would not put out false or misleading information pertaining to marijuana.

I can say the people I got to know living in that harsh environment, doing what I was doing, were the most unselfish people I have ever lived with before or since. I will be forever grateful to the people of Cahuita for giving me the support and opportunity to do what I loved to do. That can be said also for all the communities from Panama to Nicaragua that I had the good fortune to visit.

Communications

Living in Cahuita in the seventies, besides there being no electricity, there were no telephones. There were radios with batteries, which were useful as far as local and international news was concerned. Up in Limon they had an English radio station for the older black people who did not speak Spanish like me. For the few tools that they did have for communications they used them well. As far as complaints against the government were concerned, they used a lot of discretion. There were times when I thought they should have let people get on the air, but would not.

I remember when they got their first phone in the settlement. They installed it in the pub, and it was the talk of the town. That did not last long as what happened was somebody wanted to use the phone and was told they could not for whatever reason. That was the only phone for many miles, so that was a tough call to make by the pub owner. It did not go over too well in the settlement, and the phone was moved to a small shop connected to the butcher shop. That shop had a few girls living there that could speak English as well as Spanish, so it was a good fit.

Now everyone is walking around with a cell phone. So, in less than twenty years, they went from no electricity or television to walking around with cell phones. A quick leap into the twentieth century, which was understandably welcomed by the settlement.

In the seventies there was a visitor from the USA who decided to document the history of the area, the people and life in the canton of Talamanca. She got a book published with the title of What happen,

Man? which was the local form of greeting. Her name was Paula Palmer. The last I heard of her was she was teaching at the University of Colorado. The book was published in English and Spanish.

The chance bank

A business I got into while living in Cahuita was a chance bank with a local shop owner. This was about picking two numbers from 00 to 99, or three from 000 to 999. It was a great way to be fully accepted into the inner workings of the canton. It was not one of the big banks in the canton.

Before I came to Cahuita I had some experience with being what is called a number writer. Up in the USA, long before the government lottery, they had an underground lottery. The one I was involved with in the mid-fifties was a three-number pick. The odds on picking three numbers are 999-1, while the odds on picking two numbers are 99-1. There, I was a number writer, so the more money I collected the more I made off commission. The bank who had to pay on the winning number gave you the option of 15 percent of your take and paying out at 500-1, or giving you 10 percent of your take and paying out 600-1. The payout was still only 500-1, so you had some skin in the game if you only took the 10 percent off the top. That all changed when every state in the United States started selling chance.

The chance bank that we operated from Cahuita was based on two numbers from the Panama lottery which played three days a week, and the Costa Rica lottery which played on Saturday. We got most of our play from the Sunday Panama lotto. We had three sellers out doing what they do. They pretty much had the same players week in, week out. They worked off 15 percent of what they brought in and were paid 72 percent on the winning number, so the house was working on 13 percent. The sellers were not allowed to sell an unlimited amount of money on any one number, as that would put us out of business if that number played.

So, the way the system worked was the chance was sold in pieces, 4 pieces for one colon. So, if you played one colon or four pieces and it came up, you got 72 colons back. So, the more money a seller could bring in, the more pieces they could sell on any one number which we placed on half the payout.

I will tell you about one number, 52, which did not play for 12 years. There were players who had been playing that number for years, and they knew if they missed one week, 52 would play and they kept trying to put more and more money on 52, so they could get as much of their money back as possible. I know every week, number 52 was sold out by all sellers. So, it did finally play, and we took a big hit but stayed in business. A few banks went belly up and the other banks picked up their players.

The sellers knew most of their players by their number as well as their name. It was good to know what number people played in case they owed you money, and you knew when to go looking for them. They would tell you if such and such number played, come see me. So, their chance was your chance also. So that's today's lesson on a chance bank.

The action we had every day was fun, with some days more money coming in and some days more going out the door. Any profits made were put back into the settlement's sports teams equipment, maintenance of the ballpark pitch and travel expense when necessary.

This is the time when, without me even knowing, I evolved into a philanthropist. I had the good fortune to have a United States government work disability income. The income was more than enough for my lifestyle. Profits did not come into play as I was comfortable when I had a small emergency fund put up safely. That was my lifestyle for years. I did enjoy travel and a wee bit of weed to smoke. In turn I was able to procure some good weed at a fair price, to sell and get some travel money.

I was always a bit of a horticulturalist. My father had always kept a garden, so that was my start at learning plant life. While I was living down in the Costa Rican bush, there were a few plant nurseries in the area where I spent some time and talked about plants to the owners. I also spent time around nurseries in Florida, learning and talking about how to keep plants healthy and happy.

As time went on, the American community was steadily growing, with some great people with different life experiences and talents. From my memory they were all into smoking the weed. What also came into play were the magic mushrooms. I had some in a tea drink and I really did not like it. So, I pretty much stayed away from the mushrooms. When I made one trip up home to see a doctor about my epilepsy and I told him I was smoking marijuana, he gave me a strange look and wrote it up in his report, which is in my file to this day. That was a long time before they found out that the weed was very good for helping people with epilepsy, and it's possible that it had helped control my problem with seizures.

Things started to happen fast, and I became a homeowner. One of the bigger cocoa buyers in the settlement sold me an unfinished house a few hundred yards outside the center of the settlement which was much appreciated. When I left on a trip, I gave my house key to a friend from California who had a girl friend from the settlement.

Sky King

While I was gone, he moved back to California. He locked the door and left the house key with my chance partner. His girl was upset he did not give her the key. What she did was break in the back door and started taking her new boyfriends in there. That ended when a new visitor, along with his followers, moved into my house.

I had no knowledge of this as communications were not easy at this time period. This is where it gets interesting. He was living in my house with his wife and two kids, plus a small following who got very much into the magic mushrooms. The mushrooms were taking a toll on their behavior and perhaps their mental health. He would only wear a loin cloth and became a fruitarian, along with his followers. He spent a lot of time talking love, as he and his male and female followers believed in free love.

He did create fear in some people. He would do mushrooms and drink his own urine, which was a bit too much for even the most drug-tolerant community. When I returned, he left my house the same day and we talked, and he was a bit into his own world. I found him rather intelligent and not a harmful person, he moved somewhere else that I never knew. I heard stories of some cocoa farmers who would be working in their farm clearing things up, and he would be up in a tree without any clothes.

This behavior continued for a while, like perhaps a month or more. With the help of the settlement and a government official, they were all rounded up and he was put in jail. I spent quite a bit of time talking to him and thought he had mental problems, but I did not feel he was dangerous. What I felt was he was in danger because people feared him, and perhaps would take the law into their own hands. I had no problem getting him and his followers to move out of my house. I found him easy to get along with, and I think he really liked me because I did not fear him.

Jail!

When all this was going down, I was laying in my hammock on the porch one day, smoking a marijuana joint when two gentleman who I never seen before came up to me and took me into custody. The pretense was that there was a marijuana plant growing in my yard. I am sure there was, as we always cleared the pot and threw the seeds out there. When the grass got too high, I got a good friend of mine by the name of Alphonso Brown, a local fisherman. When he chopped the yard with his machete, he had great eyes and was always able to see something that was worth saving, and chop around it or transplant it. A weed is only a weed if it is growing someplace where it is not supposed to be.

My arresting officers and I made the trip up to Limon in their vehicle. When we got there, I talked to another government official, a friend that had helped me organize some sporting events. He told me they were going to put me in jail. So there I was in jail with Sky King, the name he was known by. It did not bother me as I was well used to institutional life from two years in the US Army and years on merchant ships. Also, there was nobody in the prison because of me.

I really did not know how long I would be in there, nor how long Sky King would be in there. He started to get some attention up in Limon with his followers. His new mission now was to close the jail, as it was over a hundred years old, and very crowded - 80 when I was there, in two large rooms with no beds or windows, and a small building out in the yard to defecate and urinate in, which was flushed once every morning. We had one inmate who cleared it every morning. He was the only inmate that had a job to do in there. I do not know what his compensation was or why he was imprisoned.

Another inmate I knew in there from the settlement was Freddy, who fit in down there well even though he was not a member of one of the big families who basically had control of the settlement. Freddy did not speak much English as he was Spanish. We did know a lot of the same people though. Sadly, Freddy was killed a few years later in front of his home while his young kids were there. He was killed by three young kids aged 12-14 years with a gun. They were from a very well-known family.

When you were brought into jail, they gave you a piece of cardboard to lay over the cement to sleep on. Sky King's followers would bring him in fruit every day, and the commander gave him a small knife to cut up his fruit. There were other knives in there, but I do not think they were given out by the prison commander. I did know some of the inmates from Cahuita which was nice. I spent time talking to Sky King, and all the other inmates knew I had an interest in his safety for what it was worth. I don't think Sky was sleeping much at night as he knew it was a dangerous place. He used to get some sleep during the day, and I would try and stay close.

One day out of the blue I got a visitor I did not know. He was an American from the US Embassy in San Jose. The only thing he asked me was, did I have any ID. I said yes, but I had it hidden down in the bush. How he found out I was in there, I do not know. I still do not know if he knew my name, as they had me in jail under a different name. Anyhow he said he would be back the next day, and we could go get my ID. I was looking forward to getting out the next day, just to look beyond the high walls. The next day came and nobody showed up. He never did show up again while I was in jail. It was after I had been out for a while and I was living down the fish camp.

There were three camps right along the beach and a fourth maybe fifty yards back in the swamp behind the other three. You had to walk across blocks to get to a bit of high ground. Solomon's camp is where I was staying when I was down there. He was one of the settlement's fishermen that was liked by all, who later got sick and died, I described his funeral earlier in this story. Anyway, one day I was down there, and I was over in the next camp. Whom did I see but someone who looked an awful lot like the man who came and saw me in jail. He looked at me for a second, then walked away towards the bluff where the shops were. Maybe he did come back to see me but not when I was in the lockup.

While I was still in jail, they served me with papers for growing marijuana, with a penalty of up to three years in prison. This dragged on for more than a month. It was the same routine, with few inmates leaving and a few new ones.

One day they had about eight people come in. These were some bad boys who came up from Panama. This gang from Panama were very angry lads. It was not long before piles of stuff were on fire, whatever they could get hold of was thrown in the fire. There were just two big holding tanks with over thirty to forty people sleeping in each one, on the concrete floor on a piece of cardboard. They only had one opening coming into each holding tank from the outside yard, which was surrounded by a high stone wall. The fire was outside in the yard. What I and most of the other inmates did was gather our worldly possessions, put them into a bag if we had one, and hold them tight. Some guards were talking to the rioters through the bars leading into the yard.

As it turned out, the Panama gang left the prison. Where they were going, I do not know. I would think they were escorted back to Panama. I know that Panama border down there and it's pretty porous. The chances are they had no ID. I know all the time I was down there I carried no ID as I felt I did not need it. I found people down there pretty much minded their own business and by this time I was well known in the area, so I felt I did not ever need it. On the other hand, whenever I went up to the capital of San Jose, I would carry ID. But I never carried any ID when traveling anywhere along the Caribbean coast.

The routine while in jail was food six times a day. You waited in line with whatever would hold food. I had an old coffee can that I used for all six feedings, and a spoon which I rinsed out after every use. It was coffee at 6am, porridge at 10am, main meal at 1pm, coffee at 3pm, another bite to eat at 6pm, and then something light about 9pm.

Forget about hot water. They did have an open cold-water shower and a sink to rinse some clothes.

Prison officers v. Sky King

On one Sunday they had a Christian church group paid a visit to the prison with some hymn-singers to raise our spirits. They also read some Bible verses. Sunday was an action day. It was also the day to get visitors. On Sunday we all got ice cream, to keep everyone in a good mood. Anyway on this Sunday, the officials decided that they did not want the church people and Sky King to be in the same yard. So, what they did was put Sky in isolation. It was a normal Sunday without Sky King, he was in a cell outside the yard.

After the church people left, they kept Sky in his own cell with the one light bulb. He must have done something with the wires, as the lights in the jail went out. This must have made the guards a bit upset with his behavior. From what I heard, the guards all through the night, whenever they saw him trying to sleep, they threw some cold water on him.

On Monday morning, all the new guards were standing for inspection. Sky King's cell was close and had a direct view of the inspection. What Sky done was he had a bowel movement during the night. He had a bucket in there with him and he mixed it all up with his urine. They were all standing for inspection in front of the commander in starch shirts, pants and their shoes shined to the max. This was the changing of the guards. What he did was take the whole bucket and throw it at the guards, and to put it mildly he got them good. They were not the same guards who kept him up all night by throwing cold water on him, but Sky King took the revenge he was feeling from the terrible night he had. When they took Sky King out late that Sunday morning, it was the last time I saw him.

From what I heard they injected him with Thorazine which is a pretty heavy drug that puts you in a state where you do not know your own name. I am sure they took him back home to the USA for treatment. It was a day or two after Sky King was sorted out, that I was told to pack up, and I had to leave the jail.

The gentleman that got me out, I gave him a horse I owned that he had been trying to get off me for years. His name was Lynn Potter, the oldest north American down there, he was from Montana. He spent years living in Limon where he owned a lumber business. After they built the bridge over the Estrada river and you could drive inside, he decided to build a house in Talamanca on the main highway outside Cahuita. From his business days in Limon he bought a lot of nice land inside and he wanted to be closer to it. He was in his mid-seventies at this time and had a Tico wife and two step-kids. One teenage girl and a son in the early twenties whom he thought was retarded. Potter is now buried down there in the local cemetery.

The lesson I got from the whole Sky King episode was he got into something he could not get out of and lost it. New people who came into the settlement would never hear his name mentioned. It had a sad ending, but the curtain had to come down on his show. After that episode, life went back to normal (whatever that is) in the settlement. I was back to fishing and promoting the sports and traveling up and down the coast, doing just that.

Today's date is 2 November 2019, Bridget is 9 years old today so it's party time for her and her friends at the old family homestead. A big bouncy castle was hired for the event to be enjoyed by all.

Fishing with Pete

At this time I was fishing with a local fisherman by the name of Pete. Pete was about the same age as me, and belonged to a Jehovah's Witness religious family. The reason I say this is I knew nothing about Jehovah's Witnesses. We did not talk about religion, you do learn things about the people who belong to a certain religious sect. I do not think he knew I was born and educated in the Roman Catholic Religion. Little things came out about the do's and don'ts of the Jehovah's Witness faith. Some things I found very interesting.

He did not have a motor, just a small dugout with paddles. I well remember my first fishing trip with Pete, we got up at first light, and he got some fishing gear together, a couple of lines and some fish-hooks. His dugout was down at the fish camp, so we started walking down the white beach to the camp. He was walking with his head down looking for sand crabs. He caught one and then a few more. We got down to the boat and flipped it over and dragged it down to the water's edge of what is known as the round sea. Got in the boat and paddled out about fifty yards, and Pete took out the crabs he caught on the way down to the fish camp and a small fishing hook, put a piece on there and caught what is called a bony fish - put it back down and caught another one. Then we headed out past Long Shoal. On this day the swells were not too high and Long Shoal was not breaking. If the waves were breaking, we would have had to go around the shoal.

There were about six or seven boats out that day, no motors. Just paddling up and down the shoal. It was not long before we started getting strikes, and they kept coming, we must have caught forty or fifty pounds of mackerel. We also caught a barracuda. To put it mildly, it was a great day of fishing. My hands were sore from pulling up the fishing line, as it was new to my hands. The sacrifice was well worth it, and as time went on, I got used to it. We went out fishing several times after that, but that was the best day we ever had together. Without a motor your fishing area was limited, although some fishermen had a way of rigging up a sail which gave them a bigger range.

Looking for a horse

As time went on, I bought myself a horse, as I took an interest in horses down there. It was a nice gentle riding horse named Goma, which is a slang word for hangover. Talking one day with some local friends while having a drink, we talked about going outside the settlement and buying another nice horse to bring back to Cahuita. Mario, Daniel and I departed Cahuita on the 4 am bus for Penshurst to catch the train for Limon, and on to Siquirres, where we changed trains for Guanaco. It was pretty much a full day trip.

Guanaco was very different than anyplace I have ever been. It was a junction of about five track lines with shops on both sides. It was like a wide boulevard. They were building a road into Guanaco and connecting with the main Siquirres-San Jose road. The only vehicles I could see were some big dump trucks for the road construction. Word was sent before we got here, that we were on our way to buy a horse. The next morning, there was word of a nice filly, two years old, that a

Spanish gentleman wanted us to look at. So, the three of us took a walk a little way outside to look at her. There were also a few other horses in the paddock, but that young filly looked like a nice horse. We went back to the hotel and talked horses, and there was another horse to look at the next day at another place, an old gelding. I was not really looking for a gelding, but we decided to look. It was really a nice-looking horse who would have been a better horse for winning races. We decided on the young filly and spent another night drinking and watching trains go by.

We left the horse with my chance partner's son, who was working on the road works. He sorted out train transportation for the horse as far as Penshurst. We got the next train for the trip back to Cahuita. It was a few days later when we got word that the horse was waiting for us in Penshurst, and I and two other local men made our way there. We got a dugout canoe and crossed the river to get the horse. We had the canoe and two strong men to paddle across. We walked her into the river and I held her head close by the boat as we crossed, we had to make it over to where the river bank was cut, and she would be able to make it up to the top of the river bank. We missed the cut and had to let her go, and she swam back over to the Penshurst side of the river and we had to start all over again. She was a strong young filly, otherwise she would have been taken by the current down the river to the sea.

On the second try we hit the cut and let her go, and she found her way up to the top of the riverbank. From there we had to get her to Cahuita. Earl, who was a local who was good with horses, decided to ride her there. It was about a ten-mile trip with no saddle or harness, just a blanket and a rope around her nose. There was a pub about eight miles down the road, so we decided to wait for him there. When he got there, a lot of people took a good look at her. We had a few drinks and came up with a name. My other horse was named Goma, or hangover, so this one we named after a well known Costa Rican rum drink, Cacique guaro. I was very lucky to have my fishing partner's father who was a good horseman, to take care of her. She had three healthy foals that stayed in the area.

Disability pension - reinstatement

During my time living down in Costa Rica, my government disability award had expired, and I did not reapply as I was happy and was doing good where I was. On a trip back up to the States to visit my family and check my mail (I used my sister's address while living down in Costa Rica), I found some mail there, including a letter informing me that my disability award had been terminated, as I did not reapply. I had an address down in Washington, DC, from the letter. I decided to make a trip down to DC and talk to someone. I was still not able to go back to work as an able-bodied seaman on a ship, and I had no other income.

I found the office and had the letter with me. I remember the place as being a not very large office with a lot of people working there. I gave the letter to someone who took it to the back of the office where I could not see. I did notice some people peeking around the corner looking at me though, which I thought was strange. Someone came out from the back and told me they were looking for my file. It felt like I was there waiting for a while.

Finally, someone came out and told me they found my file. They told me it was in the dead file. That's a place where they put the file waiting for someone to put in a claim for the death benefits. When they found out I was still alive and was using the same address, they assigned me another claims examiner to look at my file. I don't remember whether they even asked me where I was for those years. I do remember the gentleman's name. He was Mr. McKenna, and he told me that I would receive my back payments as I had committed no crime. I talked to several doctors and was back in the system. Mr. McKenna was good on his word and I got a check for over twelve thousand dollars. That was when I thought about making my first trip to Ireland on my way to do a circumnavigation of the big ole earth. I went back down to the bush for a spell, to get back into doing sports and a bit of business, so as to have some money to spend on sports promotion and my eventual trip round the world.

CHAPTER 3 - IRELAND, FIRST MARRIAGE

First meeting with my Irish relatives

It was the mid-seventies when I first came over to Ireland for a visit, not intending to stay. Made my way up to the northwest of the country to visit the family homestead in Carrigart, County Donegal. I just had a name, so I stayed at the Carrigart hotel. This was a genuinely nice village hotel. My family was well-known, so it was no problem finding them. While I was walking up the road from the village with my duty-free American whiskey and cigarettes, I saw someone and asked where Barney Carr lived, and I was actually close to the lane going down to the house.

I walked down the lane, and when I got a little bit down, I could see the house. I walked around the house, as that was the way the lane went. I got to the front of the house and there was a woman out feeding the chickens. She looked up at me with a confused look on her face. I told her who I was, and I knew who she was, she was my aunt Annie who was born in the same house and had lived there all her life. She was a bit shocked, as there was no warning that a visitor was coming over from the States. She went and got my Uncle Barney, the other occupant of the family homestead, who also was born there and lived there all his life.

I was invited into the house for a cup of tea. As I remember, it was a bit difficult, as it was hard for them to understand me with my Philadelphia accent, and for me to understand them with their Carrigart accent. I looked at the inside of the house - it had a big open peat fire that all the cooking was done on. It was not a big room, maybe 20 by 20 feet. Out of that 20 by 20 there was a partitioned-off small cubicle that had a window and small bed in it. That was Annie's room now. It was where her mother and father used to sleep when all the kids were growing up.

It was my grandmother who was the first one up in the morning. Her job was to get the fire going for hot water to make that first pot of tea. While she was waiting for the fire to heat the water to boiling point for the tea, she said the rosary every day. I still have those rosary beads.

Uncle Barney had his own room right off the 20x20 to his room right behind the fire. There was a third room at the other end of the cottage, about the same size as the other two, which also had a fireplace. It was not a room that got much use these days, as there were just the two of them there since their mother passed away. The fire never went out, as it was the only heat to keep them warm and cook. You had only those three rooms in a line, with an entrance door into the center room, and a door going into each of the other two rooms.

They had no indoor plumbing. They had piped water outside by the barn, so that is where they got water for cooking, washing and personal hygiene; I don't know how long they had had piped water coming down to the house. They had electricity, with two light bulbs and one electric socket. I don't know how long they had had electricity either. I would think they were one of the last to get hooked up with electricity, as they did not want any monthly bills being brought by the postman. They had one table and a few wooden chairs. As you walked inside the door, there was a small table with a water bowl large enough to wash a few cups and dishes, against the wall of the cubicle where Annie slept. The ceiling of the room was extremely high and rounded.

My father, Pat, left this house, where I was now sitting in the year of 1977, in the mid-1920s to go to the United States, where he had a brother and uncle living in Philadelphia. Annie was about 6 years old when he left, and Barney was a teenager. The other family members living in the same house then were his brothers Mark and Joe, and his sister, Mary. It would be maybe forty years before Joe, Barney and Annie would see him again. The day my father left was the last day his mother and father would ever see him, when his father got the horse and wagon hooked up to take him on the first leg of the long journey to America. The first leg of the journey to America was about a twenty-mile trip to a town called Milford, where he made connections to get to Derry, where he boarded a ship for America.

At that time there was little money or work other than subsistence farming. At the same time America was booming with plenty of work. The roaring twenties were in high gear. All you needed was a strong back and good health. A lot of the Irish made their way to foreign lands where there was work.

Traveling through Ireland

The house was not set up for guests and there was no warning of me making a trip to visit them. I stayed two more nights at the Carrigart Hotel and then was directed to a bed-and-breakfast over in Downings, which is more of a resort village. The B and B was run by another Carr family whose company I enjoyed, especially the brother of the lady who ran the place. He was what you might call my drinking partner. He also knew all the bad boys, and he could watch my back. I got back later to the house to see Annie and Barney a few times. Looking back, I think I may have been a bit disruptive to their lives, as they were not expecting a visit from their family without some advance notice. I would give them notice of my planned trip if I was to do it again. It would have made it easier for them to come to terms with.

I had a map of Ireland with me to look at and see where to go next. When I left Carrigart I made my way down to Killybegs, as that was the biggest fishing port in Ireland at the time. At that time in my life I was living like a traditional song from America, that has been recorded here in Ireland (Moonshiner), it goes like this:

'I'm a rambler, I'm a gambler, I'm a long way from home,
and if you don't like me, then leave me alone;
I'll eat when I'm hungry, I'll drink when I'm dry,
and if the moonshine don't kill me, I'll live till I die.
I've been a moonshiner for many a year,
I'll go to some hollow, I'll set up a still,
and make you a gallon for a ten-shilling bill;
I'll go to some hollow in this old country,
with ten gallon of wash, I can go on a spree.
No woman to follow, the world is all mine,
I love none so well as I love the moonshine.
Oh moonshine, oh moonshine oh, how I love thee.
You killed my poor father, but you try to kill me.
Now bless all moonshiners and bless the moonshine.
Their breath smells as sweet as the dew on the vine.
I'm a rambler, I'm a gambler, I'm a long way from home,

and if you don't like me, well, leave me alone.'
It goes on and on.

Ireland, like Costa Rica, has a high tolerance for alcohol abuse. Many people and cultures have a much different take on the subject. As for me, I think alcohol can be abused like any other mind-altering drug, if it's available for consumption, which is a social problem. As for the people who enjoy an alcoholic drink for whatever reason, they should not be deprived of that freedom. I do not believe that a government should ban the substance, as there are many people who do use alcohol responsibly and should not be punished on account of the ones who do abuse it and cause social problems for themselves and the people close to them. The ones who are most damaged by alcohol are the abuser him or herself and the people close to them.

Looking back at this period of my life, alcohol was a serious problem for me. I think also, looking back, that it was starting to make me think more about what effect it was having on my life. At the same time, I could not ever see myself giving up the drink, it was such a big part of my social life.

From Killybegs I headed south again and somehow, I ended up in a small market town called Ennistymon, in County Clare. I got a B and B there and went out for a drink. There was a little fishing village a few miles away called Doolin, which was well known in the area for traditional Irish music, and that is where night found me. I spent that night sleeping rough somewhere, and the next day after finding something to eat, someone told me about islands that you can get a boat to from Doolin, called the Aran islands. So, I went off on a small boat to an Aran island. It was a drink-fuelled few days before I got back to Ennistymon.

Meeting with Ann and eventual marriage

There, I met someone who knew a woman who was talking about opening her house as a B and B. He thought that maybe I would be interested. It sounded good to me, so he drove me back to Ennistymon, and I picked up my bag at the first B and B, where I had never slept, and moved into my new B and B. This was my first meeting with Ann, the woman I married and shared nearly twenty-five years of my life with. She had a six-year-old son, who she was raising by herself. So, I was pretty much moving into a ready-made family. Anytime you add a third person to a loving relationship, it has an effect, positive or negative. Looking back, it was negative - whether it was me or the lad, I will not lay blame anywhere, because it could have been me or him or both. The relationship between Ann and myself continued to grow, even with the signs of tension, as I thought it would improve as time went on.

It was perhaps the most passive time of my life, as I was deeply committed to the relationship and being of service to the family. I found my little niche mostly in maintaining the house and chores that we shared. It did give Ann more time to pursue activities outside the home.

I also still had my friends and family in the States and Costa Rica that I tried to maintain for as long as I could. I found it hard to keep close ties to three different countries. As time went on, I was spending more and more time in Ireland. During this time, I was also getting to know more about my father's family (four uncles and an aunt) still living in Donegal. It also gave me a keen interest in Irish history and current events that were happening at this time in Ireland.

This was the period of the most recent troubles between the north of the country, governed by England, and the south, governed by Dublin in the Republic of Ireland. It was a very polarized time in Irish history and very combustible, with many people on both sides of the divide losing their lives. The borders between the north and south were manned by the well-armed British army. During this period, I was also traveling a lot throughout Ireland, north and south. I crossed the border many times, so there were several in-your-face confrontations looking for identification. This pretty much went on all the time spent here during this period, until the three of us departed Ireland for Costa Rica in 1983.

During this period, I met and got to know some great Irish people, living in difficult times with all the troubles playing out. Migration was very strong during this period, due to the lack of jobs available in Ireland. A lot found work in the USA, Canada and Australia. That gave the country a great release for the many seeking useful employment, and the opportunity for them to send some well- appreciated funds back home to family.

Two other major events happened also during this period living in Ireland - one was that Ann and I got married in the Quaker community; and the other that my beloved father passed away. I was able to make the trip home to be with other family members to put him to rest. It was during this period in Ireland that I eventually stopped drinking alcohol, with Ann's encouragement, and I never regretted it.

Sail-boat trip

I also went over occasionally to visit friends in the US and Costa Rica, and on one of those trips, I made a great sail-boat trip with a friend of mine, Albert, from Limon to the island of San Andres, which belongs to Colombia.

This was on Albert's first sail-boat, a 45-foot sloop, which is a fair length. On the trip, there were four adults, two children, and a pit bull dog for security. The four adults were Albert and Janette, Bill Beard, who had a diving school in Costa Rica and was a very accomplished diver himself. And myself, in charge of all the gear for easy access. It was about a 200-mile trip offshore. Albert has been around boats pretty much his whole life in Florida. This was his first trip offshore in some deep water.

Me and Albert knew each other well over the years, and he knew I had spent a lot of time in deep water offshore. The trip over gave me a chance to tell of some of my long trips offshore even though this was only two hundred miles. Albert had some good up-to-date navigational equipment on the sail-boat. We had up-to-date charts, so we departed Limon and set course for San Andres. Got our night watch schedule all set up. It was easy, as we had four adults, and we set it up where we each took a two-hour watch from 10pm til 6am. After the first night, it was easy, we each got some sleep during the next day.

We did not have a good breeze, so we were only doing 4 or 5 knots, which would make it about a two-day trip. We had to make some course changes, due to the currents. We were close to the island by the second night, so we slowed down, as we did not want to try and navigate using navigational lights. I much prefer, going into a port for the first time, to do it in daylight and get a clearer picture of traffic and the inlet itself. The island is not that big, so we decided to circle the island and come into port on the far side side of the island. We had a lot of tanks and equipment for some deep diving. It was hard tacking around the north of the island, as we kept getting further and further away from the shore. So it was decided to use the motor, so as to get in a better position to use the sails again, and eventually we made it into port.

The second day we planned to do some diving. The waters were unbelievably clear and you could see deep down there. Our guide took us out to what he thought was a good spot to dive. Albert and Bill had no fear to go down beyond 100 feet of water to see what was down there. The first dive was to find some lobster for dinner that night. The guide came in handy for that. Now for some deep diving, and the guide took us to a spot that he knew of. The three of them went into the water. No way was the guide going to go as deep as Bill or Albert, he would not even go down to 100 feet. So he stayed above them when they went deep. It was the clearest water I have seen anywhere I have been.

Now the trip back to port was interesting, as I was looking at the charts to see how we were going to get back to our dock space. It seemed to me that we would have to go way to the south to get inside the reef and steer north to our dock. As we were heading south, the guide said he knew an opening that we could use to reach the other side, so we would not have to go way south. I thought he knew the waters much better than me.

As we got close to where he said the opening was, he took the wheel and I was standing right behind him. He made a turn about. Albert and Janette were down below with the two kids, and Bill was behind me. When I saw the waves building up well over ten feet, and I still could not see the opening, he was turned to starboard and started into the reef. I am standing right behind him and I am looking for this opening. Meantime, the seas are building bigger and bigger, and I still didn't see this opening he was talking about. I was thinking about the two young kids down below and I decided to take the wheel from him. I looked to the port and starboard and decided to go to port. I gave it full power and turned the wheel hard to port, so I got the boat turned around heading back out to the open sea.

You have to make those calls quickly, and Bill said to me he was glad I took the wheel, which made me feel better about my making the move. When I gave it full power and made the turn the boat did roll a bit. Albert put his head out of the galley to see what was happening and he saw us coming out of the roll, and looked over the stern at the big seas behind us. The guide and all of us were quiet for the rest of the trip back to the dock.

After we docked, we picked up a local deep sea diver from the island who was supposed to know the waters. Albert also had a visit from his uncle who lived on the mainland of Colombia, and could easily get a flight to the island. At that point, we had about as many people on there as you would want, without being on top of one another.

The big thing I got out of this trip was I got to talk to Bill a lot. He told me he had stopped drinking eight years ago and had no problems with it. I never really thought about joining (AA) Alcoholics Anonymous, which I have heard about. I am sure other people have done it, but it was just that I have never got to know of a group. What it did do is give me hope that it is possible. As I said earlier, I had never in my wildest dreams thought I could stop drinking. It was so intertwined with my social life that it would just not be possible. What Bill gave me was something you could never put a value on, which is hope. It has been close to or more than forty years since I stopped putting alcohol into my body, which freed me from that mind-altering stuff.

We spent three days on the island and I did do some drinking, but not with Bill. One day I was out, and there were some military trucks out picking up young men. I asked what they were picking the men up for, and the locals said they were being inducted into the Army. It happened to me up in the States, why not here also, except I got a letter with the time and place to report.

It was a great trip with some great people. When we got back to Limon, we had to clear customs and immigration. Customs came on the sail-boat, we were waiting on deck, and Janette had all the portholes closed - it got hot down there with all the portholes closed, so the customs gave it a quick search. It also came up when I was leaving Costa

Rica, when immigration checks your passport, and they saw that I had a stamp for San Andres island and an entry stamp for Limon. The immigration officer asked me a lot about the stamps.

Move to Costa Rica as a family

During the early eighties, I really wanted to spend some more time down in Costa Rica, and Ann agreed we could maybe spend some time as a family down there. It took quite a bit of planning as we had to dismantle the home and leave all in one go. Her plan was to spend some time living in a Quaker community in Monteverde, Costa Rica.

This was a very interesting community settled by a group of Quakers who were not pleased with the US involvement in the Korea conflict, where my brother proudly served a tour of duty as a draftee in the US Army. The Quakers of Monteverde were a brave and hardy bunch, who traveled by land from Alabama and other States. They brought with them a herd of milking cows. They already had purchased a very large parcel of land, many hectares way up in a tropical cloud forest. Title to the land was very clear, so coming from the U.S., you would think that was it. But there were many people living on the lands that were unknown at the time to the Quakers. So when they took possession of the lands, they found out other people were also on pieces of the land, that they were working without the previous owner's knowledge. They were what are called 'precaristas' (squatters) in Costa Rica.

I have seen this happen in Costa Rica. It's a legal process to get them off the land that you have purchased. It ends up with having to buy the land a second time, and keeping people from taking possession, so as to deal with it quickly, before they can plant the lands and build shelters for themselves and their family. Large landowners have problems with squatters, but the other side of the problem is that land is unavailable to poor people who cannot afford to buy it, and can only look for land that is just not being used. All the time I was down there, you would see landowners with a horse and a rifle over their shoulder. It happens often where there are large tracts of land that cannot be secured.

Access to this land was very difficult, to put it mildly. When they settled in, the Quakers found out they were so far from the market to sell their milk that they had no choice but to make cheese. To this day, that cheese is most sought after throughout the country. There is much more info on this settlement on the Quaker web site.

Back in Ireland, all the connections were made for accommodations and school for Ann's son. So now it was just sorting out the house, packing up, buying airfare tickets and making arrangements to bring our beloved Springer spaniel dog, Patsy, with us. The next time I would return to Ireland to live again would be November 1999.

Me and my beloved springer spaniel, Patsy, departed first for the USA. Ann and Damon stayed back to sell what was left, like my car and household items. She found a good neighbor to sort the cottage out. A tenant was found, which did not work out well, as no rent was ever paid. That tenant was sorted, and a new tenant was found who really worked out well. He ended up buying the cottage some years later.

After I picked up Ann and Damon at the airport, we got it together to make our way down to Costa Rica by air. The thing I remember most about arriving down in CR is the warm reception we got from all my mates down there. It was agreed that I would mostly stay down the Caribbean side of the country, and the other half of the family would spend their time in the cloud forest with the Quaker community.
I bought a pickup truck so I would have transportation to get around the country without depending on public transport, which is good but slow.
Ann and Damon did not get down often to my stomping grounds as the area did not go well with her. She very much preferred living in the cloud forest with the Quaker community. They had a house up there that suited. I used to try and split my time between the two homes.

The boxing club

During that period, I got back into sports promoting and went into organizing a boxing club, for which the local community gave me a lot of support. It was a lot of fun and very entertaining for the whole zone, as I traveled from Limon to the Panama border doing the promoting, so there was no problem finding venues.

To put it together, I needed to find some funds. Since I had been away from the settlement, my chance bank had closed, as my partner had passed away. I found another well-established business family to set up my chance bank again, my sellers came back to me, and I got a new seller from another settlement, to help raise funds. Back in action and having fun.

Then I needed help finding some training equipment and setting up the boxing ring. Word travelled throughout the zone that I was looking for lads who were interested in joining a boxing club. The lower weight classes were easy to find, the higher the weight were more difficult. There was a boxing club up in Limon, and I did know people up there who did some boxing promoting. There were people in the settlements who did have some ring experience and would do a few expeditions. I also talked to some people from the European and North American communities that had built up in the area since the road opened, to see if any of them were interested. I did not get any bites out of the Europeans, but I did get some help from a North American, a lad from Florida who did some club boxing and was interested. I found some local sports people who would act as trainers, and set up some sparring sessions. My main motive was on the club level, for Olympic possibles. Finally, I just had to set up some exhibition boxing matches. There were some older people in the area who had boxing experience.

This was the first time living in the settlement where I had my own pickup truck for transport. It made things a bit easier and quicker to put the pieces together. During this time they were also pushing a road through from Puerto Viejo to Manzanillo, and it was nearing completion - this opened up a large coastal area of Talamanca to visitors. The last time I had been through Manzanillo with the horses and knowing the lay of the land, I did not think this road would go any further south along the coast. The talk down in Monkey Point was that if they did push a road in to there, it would come from Bridgefoot, where a new road heads south to Panama and north to Limon.

But it was not too long before the road opened, and the people of Manzanillo decided to have a fiesta to celebrate the opening of the road. For entertainment they built a ring, and asked me to bring down boxers for the entertainment.

There was one gentleman by the name of Wagoner (known to everyone as Waggie), who I and everyone else in the settlement had been listening to for years, telling me how tough he was, as he danced around doing some shadow boxing. So I told him I had a fight for him down in Manzanillo for the grand opening of the road. He said he would do it if I bought him a new pair of runners. I was looking forward to driving down there, as the last time I was down that far was with Cockeye and the horses.

Waggie was a classic bush man, as he could blend into the jungle just like those big cats. You did not see him too much in the settlement since he stopped living there. His mother left him a nice cocoa farm that he managed until the sickness came in and wiped it all out. He sold the farm to all his friends at well below the market price, so he was well liked and entertaining. Everytime he came into the settlement he would go to the pubs and start chatting to someone who did not know him, and then he would tell them it's his birthday today, and believe me or not he got a lot of birthday drinks, for he had a lot of birthdays.

The day of the big fight I had my pickup truck ready for the trip. My friend Billy was with me and he offered to be Waggie's corner man for the bout. That was the same Billy who I was fishing with up in Tortuguero when Marta had her second baby. We left the settlement with the back of the pickup packed to the max.

A road opening is always interesting, as it opens up an area that people would not otherwise get to. After we got past Puerto Viejo a bit, we were on the new road on our way to Grape Point where there was a small settlement, and then on to Manzanillo. The road was a dirt track, and being new it did not have many pot-holes yet. I knew there were two big inclines to climb before Manzanillo. We got up the first and started going down, and they had built a wooden bridge to connect the two hills. This wooden bridge had no sides just some planks of wood connecting the two ends. I made it across the bridge and started heading up the hill on the other side, where we made a big turn and started heading down into Manzanillo. I have been down to Manzanillo before by dugout canoe and on the foot and animal trail. But this road took a different track for some reason.

Manzanillo is not big and had no roads, just trails. Maxie had the only shop and pub. Maxie had done a great job clearing out some space for the ring and parking for my truck and a bus from Puerto Viejo - most of the people were from the surrounding area who came by foot, horse or mule. Along with Waggie, representing Cahuita, was another boxer, the kid from Puerto Viejo who later made it up to Guatemala to compete for the world Olympics representing Costa Rica.

They had plenty of food, music and guaro. It was a festive occasion, with a lot of people gathered to celebrate the new road reaching this far south in coastal Costa Rica. There were a few more local lads doing some bouts. While they were happening, a few out-of-ring fights broke out among the women who were present, which got into some pretty heavy hair-pulling competition. All this time, Waggie wanted to know who he was going to fight and I did not know, until I talked to Maxie and he told me. It was some fighter from Panama, who, by the word going around, was a professional. Waggie was in the ring when the fighters where being announced and he found out. He was ready to jump out of the ring and Billy called me over and we talked; I said I didn't believe it and that they are just trying to get you scared, which they did do. I calmed him down as best I could, and told him if it was true the fight will not last long.

Then they rang the bell and Waggie was not going to get out of the corner, until Billy pushed him out. Both fighters are in the center of the ring. Waggie started his dancing and shadow boxing, and the Panamanian started to throw some punches and Waggie avoided most of them, and some were glancing blows. He made it through the first round of a four round fight. Billy himself was a good sportsman and he told Waggie how good he was doing. Waggie still did not have the confidence he needed to beat this guy. The first half of the second round was the same, Waggie dancing and dodging most of the blows, and some glancing blows landing but not really hurting Waggie. Waggie then started to throw some punches and I was very surprised how good his timing was, as he did land some. I was happy to see him get through two rounds and I could tell he was starting to feel more in control, with the confidence level looking better. You could see the crowd getting more into the fight. Waggie had all the fans from Cahuita and some from Puerto Viejo and the area south of there.

I knew the third round had to be a round where a good fighter prepares for the last round, and paces himself to have something left for the last round. I really thought by this time he would not be able to keep his hands up and was not feeling hopeful. The bell rang for round three and the Panamanian came out of his corner quickly - was it just show? Waggie was defending himself well, slipping most punches and showing some good foot work. With some landing, but really not hurting Waggie. It takes more energy to throw and miss a punch than it does to land a punch. That started to show. I could also see the Panamanian starting to suck air with his mouth open, which was not a good sign for him. The second half of the round, the Panamanian went into defense mode and I could see Waggie coming on strong. That was the first round he won. By this time the crowd was very much into the fight.

This is the round that we will see who has what left in his tank - round four. Both competitors came out quickly, just show maybe. The Panamanian started with a quick flurry of punches that Waggie was able to defend against, then got his second wind and controlled the fight, but did not have enough in the tank to finish the Panamanian with a knockout. There is a saying you learn while living in this zone, that bushmen never get tired. For one bushman I saw perform that day, that is sure true. It was some great entertainment to be able to be a small part of.

It was starting to get late in the day and I had to get all my passengers back to Cahuita. It was like trying to round up cats, as there were some very happy Waggie supporters. We did get a downpour of rain but it did not last long. As soon as the rain stopped, they were all ready to head back home. I loaded up the truck and headed up the hill. With all the weight in the back I got enough traction to get up the hill. When I made the turn at the top and started heading down on the wet muddy road, I told everyone in the back not to move about. I had the truck in low gear and pumping the brakes, staying focused on the road and the wooden bridge I had to get across. It was what I would call blue-knuckles driving. I got across the bridge, which was the big danger. I had enough traction to get up the next hill and down again, and back onto level road leading into Puerto Viejo and all flat road back to Cahuita. Waggie did not have to buy a drink in Cahuita for a week nor tell strangers that it was his birthday !

So it all went well, with one young man from the zone making it up as far as Guatemala for the semi-finals of the Olympics. That alone made it all worthwhile.

Move to the States

What did happen while we were down there was that the airline Air Florida had a bad crash and a lot of people lost their lives. They then went into bankruptcy, so our return tickets pretty much became worthless. Our funds were running low, and money was not available to purchase new tickets. Ann, with her great language skills (English, Russian, French, and now add fluency in Spanish to the list), found work in the capital, San Jose, where she earned enough money to purchase return tickets to Philadelphia. She also got her son registered to attend Quaker boarding school in Westtown, Chester County, Pennsylvania, for his further education.

This time period was a difficult time for us with money. My family in the Pennsylvania area gave me a bit of help to make it through. At this time, we had nothing but what we brought back from CR. We found a two-room apartment that permitted kids and dogs in a big complex outside West Chester, Pa. We had a lot of help from different sources to get the place sparsely furnished with used furniture.

When we first settled in the US, there were immigration issues for Ann and Damon as far as obtaining the Green cards for residency. Ann was always very good at sorting out these kinds of problems, but this was too much even for her. She found some help with a non-profit immigration help organization. This office in Philadelphia was an hour away by bus. What also happened here was she got a job in the same organization as a trainee employee. This was what eventually led her to take a law degree from the University of Delaware, specializing in immigration law.

First years in Central Pennsylvania

We stayed in West Chester for about two years, until we bought a real nice two-bedroom house in Peach Bottom, southern Lancaster County. This was mostly Amish and Old Order Mennonite farm country. The Amish are a very interesting religious community who are governed very tightly by the local bishop. It was a great opportunity for me to get to work with and get to know community members. Their work ethic is of the highest I have ever seen. Ann was working in a branch office of her immigration assistance organization in Lancaster City. We lived there for several years, did some major reconstruction work, and sold the house and bought a house twenty miles up the road in Lancaster City itself, and were back to city living.

While this was all happening, I was in a good position to spend three or four days a week with my mother, who was in the advanced stages of Alzheimer's, living in her retirement home in Villas, NJ, so this was a great opportunity for me to give back to my beloved mother. It was me and another gentleman friend who loved her also, who shared the time. If things came up where I could not do the time needed, my brother John would take time off work to fill in for me. This went on for years until winter was coming and the disease was advancing. The fear was she would wander out in the freezing weather and freeze to death which was not acceptable. It was very difficult for me to put her into a nursing home, even though it was the best choice I had. It was only a short time later that she passed away with a heart attack.

Something to know about her is that she was a very strong woman who spent over thirty years of her life as an office cleaner, working from five to eleven each weekday night. She was never hospitalized, except for the birth of her first child. I believe that, because of her strength and her tendency to wander, she was drugged to a point where it influenced her heart. I say this because I took her to the doctor for her illness, and all the doctors told me she had a strong heart for a woman her age. But I do not feel that it was wrong to put her in a home, as it was a humane way to end the very full life of a very sick person, who would only suffer and deteriorate more.

The void that this put into my life was filled with getting a garden and doing some fishing for the meat. I very much enjoyed growing food and catching fish to cook for dinner. My life during this time was not as exciting as in Costa Rica, but at the same time enjoyable and personally rewarding. At this time, we both had different life paths - I was more of a house-husband which is a dead-end path, and Ann was on a new career path which I think we were both happy with. All during this time, Ann was also exploring all types of religious communities and groups, which I had no problem with, and I found it interesting on a spiritual and informational level. I was also very happy and content with my own religious beliefs and spiritual life. I was there just as support for her interests, as I would never have explored all these religious cults myself. I did find it all very educational though, as to what type of communities are out there in this world. More about some of these later.

<u>Dogs and dog-breeding</u>

It was during this period that my best companion, Patsy the Springer Spaniel was getting older and could not continue having puppies. She was one great bitch, who was also a great mother to all her pups, which made her a pleasure to work with when she had her pups. Springer Spaniels make great pets and are also great working dogs for bird hunters. I always tried to find a home for at least two pups in her litter with people who would train them to work. My thinking on this was going back to the French poodle - at one time a great working dog - which has been bred out of its working capacities, and is now just another pet dog. I did not want this to happen to another great working breed of a dog.

Before Patsy died, I started to think about restocking some breeding stock of Springer Spaniels. As Patsy was such a great dog, I decided to look for some breeding stock in Ireland, as I was looking to do a visit over there anyway to visit family and friends. I had already acquired Alfonso, a pure-bred Springer, from a local breeder in Maryland.

I got in touch with the American Kennel Club to find out some info on the Irish Kennel Club, and how to transfer dogs from one country to another. I then got in touch with the Irish Kennel Club to see who was breeding Springer Spaniels. I got some good leads, and had to choose a time when to make the trip and bring some pups back with me. I had a two-week window between 6 and 8-week-old puppies. I did put a trip together and remember this was all before I even thought about computers and email. While I was in Ireland, I found some nice puppies to bring back, one each from two different litters. They both came from good stock. While I was over there I got up to Donegal to see the family and let them know how I was doing, and give them news on the rest of the family in the USA.

To get the puppies back to the US, I had to take them to a vet and get a good health certificate on them. As they do not have any rabies in Ireland or England, and the pups were traveling to the US where there is rabies, I asked about a rabies shot for them. They said they did not have rabies or rabies shots, which made sense. All I had to do now was get my friend Robert Crosbie to make a dog kennel for the plane trip back to the US. That done I was ready to move. The trip back went well, though I did have to go to a different area of the airport to pick up the pups. Overall, the trip went well and I got to talk to some knowledgeable dog people. I also spent some quality time with some good friends. When I got them to the US, I had to change all their documents to the US Kennel Club format, which went smoothly.

With four dogs I needed to make a fenced-in dog area, which was sorted with the help of my cousin's son and his helper, who put up a good secure fence and a nice large dog house. I wanted to wait until they got to be a year old before I started to breed them. I got them their rabies shots, and enjoyed working with them. One was on the small side for a Springer, so I named her after a bantam rooster, Banty. The other was named Lady.

Banty was the first to have a litter and it was a difficult one, as she took a bad infection in her tits, which caused problems. She had plenty of milk but I could not let her stay with the puppies, as they would have made the skin opening much worse then it was. I took her to the vet, who was very good. The vet started her on a series of shots, which meant I had to take her there every morning and carry her in the back door and out after she got her shot. While I had her and the pups at home, I had to bring the pups to her every four hours to let them nurse, while I pressed paper towels over her open wound until they had their fill and she was also relieved. This went on for a week, every four hours I would do this. It was pretty intense, but what I can say is we did not lose any of the puppies and the mother had a full recovery. With all my sleep interruptions I did have dreams about dogs.

Dog Days

Barney with Patsy in Ennistymon

Barney at Peach Bottom, with new arrivals from Ireland

Patsy's first litter of eleven pups, in Ennistymon

With Alfonzo in Peach Bottom

Next generations of Springer pups

With four full-grown dogs, I always tried to spend at least a couple of hours a day with them. Another problem came to light when I had Alfonso checked for hip dysplasia, which is a real problem when breeding healthy pups. You cannot get them checked for that problem until they are a least a year old, when it shows up in the x-ray. When I had him checked, sure enough it came back positive. The first person I called was the breeder I bought Alfonso off, and then I called all the ones who got his puppies. I said I was sorry, but they should know not to breed any of the pups, as it would only pass the problem on to other dogs. This dysplasia is a very serious problem in dog-breeding, as it will take maybe five or six years before it shows up, and by that time the dog or bitch could have had many pups, which only makes the problems worse.

I had Alfonso castrated and passed him on to a nice home as a nice pet. Now I was down to three dogs, but then I also lost Banty to the road, as she must have chased something across the road and was hit by a speeding car or truck. So now I was down to two dogs, Patsy and Lady, plus two of Banty's pups It was not really going well for me, and I decided to get out of the dog-breeding line of work.

I found a nice home for Lady, a hunting camp down in north western Florida. I planned a trip where I took Lady and Banty's two puppies with me down to North Carolina to see David Feerick's brother, Johnny, to drop one off there. I left Peach Bottom in late afternoon, and didn't get to northern North Carolina till close to midnight, so I found a motel and got about four hours sleep. We left there at 4 am for Charlotte, North Carolina to drop off a pup for Johnny and his son, Tommy. We got there about 8 am, and had a really big breakfast cooked up by Johnny.

From there on to a north-western Florida hunting camp to drop off Lady, who was ready to have her pups. I arrived there early evening and got a good meal. It was a really cold night for that part of the country and I still had snow in the bed of my truck. Everyone stared at the snow, as they do not see it that often, if at all. The camp was not really set up for cold weather. They had one wood stove in the middle of the room. The windows was not very air tight and you could feel the cold air coming in.

A place was made up for Lady, as I knew she was ready to start having her litter. She gave birth to seven beautiful healthy pups. She was not being a good mother and was very confused as this was her first litter. Me and some others stayed with her, coaching her to clean them up and let them suck, but at first it was not happening. The pups were making a lot of noise. Eventually she did start to accept the pups and do what she was supposed to do.

I slept the night with Banty's pups, and spent the next day riding around muddy roads with a lot of deep water holes to navigate through using the four wheel drive. These were ideal conditions for deer and wild hogs, and they had quite a few dogs that they used to run the animals. It was a fun day out in the woods looking for game. The camp is on the edge of hundreds of acres of planted out trees.

The next morning I was back on the road with one pup left to care for. The whole trip from north-west Florida to Gainesville in central Florida, there was a thick layer of ice covering all the plants the whole six hour trip. The cold does not usually come that far south. I got to my friend's house with the puppy, a birthday present for one of his daughters which worked out well. I then found out Joe was not in Orlando, but had a new trailer in another park. I found the park and the trailer and he told me him and Mary, his wife, had a dispute as he wanted to leave Orlando. So here I am, just me and Joe on Christmas Day, having a Christmas dinner of baloney lunch meat sandwiches that we both enjoyed immensely. Total freedom for both of us, although temporary. He told me at that time that perhaps some people are just meant to live by themselves. That separation did not last long, as they both decided to live in the trailer they had together, in Cape Canaveral, Florida. That is where they spent their final years together in happiness.

After taking Lady to her new home in Florida, we were back down to our first Springer, Patsy, who was getting up in years. Nobody grows old by themselves. It was not long before she developed her final bout of cancer, and had to be put down. It was a real loss for all of us as she was so much part of our life.

Round the world on a train

After we had moved to Lancaster County, I also made a very interesting trip around the world by train, flying across the Atlantic and Pacific oceans. I departed Newark, New Jersey, airport for Shannon, Ireland. I spent a week or so visiting friends and family in Ireland, before boarding a ship to make the crossing to Le Havre, France. I took a train up to Paris from there, then a train up to Brussels, Belgium, where I got to visit Ann's brother, who lived there. From there I took a train across Europe to Budapest, Hungary.

I was not able to book the train from Budapest to Moscow in advance, for whatever reason. I stayed in Budapest for a week before I left on a midnight train for Moscow. There was a three-hour layover at the Russian border, where they had to lift the train carriage off its wheels and put it back on other wheels, as the track gauge is different in each country. While there, I was questioned by a Russian officer (who spoke perfect English), asking me about money, drugs and guns, and he seemed satisfied with my answers. This was a pretty bleak border crossing, and I asked how he got posted in this god-forsaken place. His answer was 'It's a long story!'

The train got into Moscow about five hours later where I was met by a guide who brought me to my hotel. I had a few days before my booking on the trans-Siberian train to Beijing, China. While in Moscow I purchased some Russian rubles. To tell the truth there was very little to buy. I think that Russians have a lot of rubles, with the only problem being, there were very limited numbers of items they could buy. The opposite of where I was coming from, where there was so much stuff that you could buy, but not enough money.

The time of year I made this trip was in February, so it was the coldest time of year to make the trip. The train left Moscow at midnight and made many stops. I was shown to my cabin that I shared with a fellow traveler, who was from Japan. They had two classes, hard and soft - hard had four occupants, and soft had two occupants. There were four of us in our cabin making the trip. Myself, a young English lad making his way down to Australia, an Austrian woman who was on her way to Korea to teach, and the Japanese gentleman who refused to fly to get back home. Representatives of the allied forces and the axis powers, who would never have shared a cabin together during the Second World War. We all had our connections booked to move on from Beijing on the next leg of our journey.

I found the most interesting part of the crossing was Lake Baikal and the area round the city of Irkutsk, which I really felt I would like to return to and explore in the summer. It's an area of Russia that has some great history and, I would think, people. Our guide on the train was from Irkutsk so she departed the train there. I still had a few rubles, so I passed them on to her for her great company during the trip.

We still had a day or two before we crossed the border into China. At that border they also had to change engines and food service cars. I got to get off the train for a while to do some shopping, and they had a really nice fur vest there that I would have bought, but they would not let it leave the country. I finally found something that I would like to buy, and they would not sell to me! So be it, life goes on. We also had a Russian gymnast team on the train that was expecting to compete in China. Sad to say, for some reason they were not permitted to enter China.

On the trip through northern China to the capital we picked up more passengers. There was a group of men with their North Korean dress. I looked at them as they would have been about the same age as my brother, who served a tour in Korea during the conflict - I was thinking they were also across the line from where my brother was. Just a thought. I made this trip shortly after the Tiananmen Square protests(1989). China at the time was a bit hostile towards Westerners. The hotel in Beijing had very few guests, in fact I think there were more employees than guests. I spent three days in the hotel, and I went out and about with my newfound Japanese friend from the train, as he was also waiting for the ferry to take him back to Japan. We did get some strange looks - whether they thought he was Chinese touring with a Westerner I do not know.

My next train trip was heading south to the southern border with Hong Kong, which was a three-day train trip. I did not see any other Westerners on that train. There was no one I could speak to at all for three days, which is rather strange. There were some young Chinese passengers who tried to practice their English on me. That was not easy, as their English was not easy for me to understand – so it was a bit embarrassing for both of us. In the dining car they did manage to find me a fork and spoon to eat with. It was a great trip through the Chinese countryside, where now and then you could see a dog. There are no dogs in the cities or towns of China, you must get far out in the country to see dogs.

When that three-day leg of the train journey ended in Guangzhou, I was now pretty much back in the tropics. Now I had to find the ferry that would take me over to Hong Kong, to fly across the big Pacific Ocean to Seattle, Washington, to board an Amtrak train for Chicago. I stayed in that southern city for a few days before boarding the ferry to Hong Kong. One thing I do remember about getting on the ferry was meeting two couples from Australia. By this time, it was a long time since I had any meaningful conversation in English. I heard them speaking English and I went over and joined them. I sat down at their table and started talking and talking and talking. As I look back, they must have thought I was 'loony'! I just wanted to talk to someone.

I spent a week in Hong Kong just using the public transportation and going through the markets. The one thing that I noticed right away was the number of people who were very active on their mobile phones. In 1989, there were not many mobile phones in the USA. This was the first time I had seen people using their mobile phones on public transport. It was also good to see people out walking their dogs again, and being able to enjoy an American McDonalds for hamburgers and breakfast. Now for the Transpacific air crossing to the next series of trains, this time belonging to Amtrak.

Planes and airports are boring with large numbers of people who are thinking more about where they are going, than where they are now. Got to Seattle the next morning and went directly to the Amtrak station. For some reason, it was not possible to get a seat on the Empire, which is the train that I wanted to travel in across the entire north of the country to Chicago. In order to get the Empire, I would have to wait until the next day. I was glad to wait, as that is the train that I wanted. It was some great scenery across the mountains of

Washington and into Idaho. What I noticed particularly was the landscape, which was very similar to Siberia - a frozen desert with little water. They have the same situation across a lot of the states along the Canadian border, water is in short supply.

The trip was going well until we got into Montana to a stop called White Fish, where we were stopped - there was a derailment with a train coming from the opposite direction loaded with automobiles. It seems like we waited for hours, until Amtrak decided to bus people around the derailment to board the other Amtrak train from Chicago to Seattle that was also blocked. That operation went smoothly, and we were all happy to be rolling again. What it did mean was, I missed my connection from Chicago to Lancaster, Pa. It meant a night in a Chicago hotel, paid for by Amtrak which was pleasant enough.

The next day I boarded my last train on this trip round the world. I got into Lancaster the next afternoon, after leaving traveling east and returning traveling east. It was a once-in-a-lifetime trip. The only train delay was the derailment with Amtrak. I still think Amtrak is a very good long-distance train service.

Golfing

It was now time to get back into my home routine with the cooking and shopping. It was spring, and time to start planning the garden for the spring and summer. Spring was always my favorite season, as it was like a new beginning, plus also the best time of year for sports, with the college basketball tournaments and spring training for all of baseball. It was around this time I started getting into playing golf.

A lawyer friend of Ann's had a husband who was very much into golf, and we talked, and I decided to take up the game. The first thing I did was look up a pro to take some good lessons, so I would not get into bad habits which would be hard to break. I got a set of used clubs, went out to a small golf club, set the tee, grabbed my driver and took the grip and let it rip. I really enjoyed the game and was golfing as many as five weekdays a week. I bought a membership in the club and found some great golfing mates. The one that I found to be the most interesting character was a second world war army veteran in his eighties, who had some really great stories and was a fun guy to golf with. We never really kept score when we were playing amongst ourselves, as we discovered that it really did not take away from the pleasure of the game. It was fun and great exercise.

There are two stories I remember from Harry: one is when it was just me and him playing one afternoon; when we got to the 17th fairway where it has a bit of hill going up to the green, I said to Harry 'I am getting a bit tired', and he said that this was his second round of the day. I never said to him I was tired again!

Harry played two rounds every day that weather permitted. We were out golfing this one day, and he said after he got home after the second round of golf, he decided to get down to the river and do some fishing. Anyhow he was walking out into the river, and somehow he slipped and fell in the mud. He made his way back home, and his wife looked at him; so he told her what happened, and she said 'you are just like a little kid'. To me that is something I would love to be called in my eighties while playing golf and fishing. He was just a great golfing partner.

I continued to play golf while living in Lancaster later, and for a short period when I moved back to Ireland, before it became too difficult and I had to sell my clubs. It was a great run though. I did fall into a pretty comfortable and healthy lifestyle with the garden, fishing and golf. I still feel that my house-husband role of cooking, shopping and keeping the yard looking good was also very rewarding.

I also used to like to get down to Florida for spring training in the last two weeks of March. All the clubs pretty much had the teams together that they were going to take north for the opening of the season in April. They always have a few players who are under scrutiny, to see whether they were going to make the team or go back to a minor league team and work to improve, or wait to see if someone is put on the injury list and they get the call to come to the big dance. All teams are very optimistic that time of year thinking it could be their year to win a World Series in October.

Ann at law school

All this time Ann's career path was moving forward. When she decided to pursue her law degree, she needed her higher education school records from Liverpool University and Oxford University in England which went back a few years. Time went on and she never received a reply. Meantime she continued with the process of applying which included the LSAT exam, and some writing. Apparently, they were impressed with her writings, enough that she was accepted into the University of Delaware Law school without her school grades from England. This I found quite impressive. Attending law school was a very busy time in her life while maintaining part-time employment and attending school at night with all the travel time and studies. She did hold up very well. I was concerned that she would get run down and get sick which did not happen. I gave her my full support all through this busy time in her life. She did graduate fifth in the class of a hundred, and got the Pro Bono award, which was also quite impressive.

Now for the hard part, the Pennsylvania lawyer bar exam. After a lot of studies, she passed, and now she had to look for a law firm to sponsor her and give her a job. There was a fine lawyer in Lancaster who always tried to help women lawyers find an opening in a male-dominated profession. He gave her an office, and she was now practicing immigration law at the ground level. Life settled down a bit after that, and Ann continued her exploration of Christian religious communities with some strange twists and turns.

Soup kitchen community

There were two that I do remember well: one was for the purpose of helping the homeless. This was in Atlanta, Georgia on Peach Street, a main street in Atlanta. It was a big house purchased by two ministers who decided to devote their money and lives to helping the homeless. I found this to be a very good cause. They would let the homeless sleep in their yard. They would go out in the early morning with loads of food to feed the homeless in Atlanta. They also had showers for them, and would give them a change of clean clothes. They served free lunch to a lot of needy people. Another good service that they provided to the homeless who wanted to get help was a postal address, as we all know if you do not have an address, people do not want to even talk to you. Some of their staff were brought in from the streets to work and live inside. It was an alcohol-free house. One gentleman who was brought inside to work told me he was at the door letting people in to eat lunch. He told me he never refused anyone, as he thought it could be Jesus himself testing him. We spent one week down there and found it very interesting, but it was not a place I would devote my life to, which you had to do if you wanted to join that community. There are other good things I do that I would not be able to keep up with.

Bruderhof community

The other one was called the Bruderhof (they used the original German word). This community was formed in Germany prior to World War II and Hitler. They also had some English members in the cult. They picked up everything and moved to England. They settled in England and the war started to heat up. England was concerned about the German nationals in the cult, so they were given about two thousand acres down in Paraguay, South America, to do their own thing.

They accepted the offer and boarded a ship for Paraguay. The land they were given, I would think is up near a border with a neighboring country, to build up the border area to prevent incursions from their neighbors. They built three settlements, one with a hospital, one for growing food, and another for manufacturing. I know from my time living in the jungles of Central America just how hard that can be for a relatively small group with little or no outside support. It did become too much for them to keep it together with all the infighting. In order to keep the cult intact, they had to do something. They found another religious group either the Mormons or Mennonites that bought the settlements off them. These were much bigger organizations with no problem getting outside support to maintain the settlements.

With the funds they received, they got US visas and moved to the southern United States as a unit. Each member could take one duffel bag of belongings with them on the ship up to the USA. It's a community that if you decide to join, you give up a lot and it's up to you if you think you get enough in return. You must sign all your worldly possessions over to the organization, and if you later decide to leave, they will give you a small sum of money. If they have work for you to do outside the settlement, they will give you the necessary funds. All or most of the positions of authority are held by long-standing members. It is completely drug-free, as money does not change hands within the community. It is a very institutional lifestyle. Perhaps the earthly attractions are security, as I think women join in bigger numbers than men do. I also believe they must recruit new members for no other reason than to keep the gene pool in the settlements at a healthy level. There is much to learn about these cults which is hard to do, as they are very suspicious of outside involvement.

There is also a group made up of ex-Bruderhof members, who organized themselves to assist others who for whatever reason decided to exercise their only freedom - that is to leave and go on the road. I believe these types of community are very good for the membership who are high up in the ranks of leadership positions. Like the top leader who has his own airplane. There must be a message there, when the cult members living inside have only one freedom, that is to leave with little in your pocket. They do manufacture some quality goods for the disabled. It would be very hard for an outside manufacturer to compete with them, as all labor is free, except for room and board and health care.

I would also like to say that it is right that these cults should benefit from freedom of religion. You also must know they operate like a government within a government, with much secrecy that should be monitored. I am sure they have dealings with the government for benefits like Social Security, which I found out is collected by the members when they are of age or disabled. They must pay their required quarters to collect. Even though they pay their quarters they do not receive a paycheck, so they must dance around that one somehow. When they get their SS check they don't keep it. From my experience spending time in the cult, I found them to be happy enough and just wanting to be left alone to do their thing in peace. They still deserve watching, as they could spin out of control in a heartbeat, like other cults have.

Ann joins the Catholic Church

Ann was still moving along with her studies and doing well. She was still looking into religious communities and holding meetings at different houses of a group that was formed of similar-minded people who were also looking. This small group also morphed into sort of a social group. They were all from different larger religious groups. This is going back as much as 30 years, and Ann lost touch with most of them when she finally converted to Catholicism.

Catholicism is known as the mother church, and all the other Christian churches came about as a schism or a schism from a previous schism. This happened in all organized religious groups with a long history, whether it be Islam, Hinduism or Buddhism, there are many different sects. I have been very fortunate to be able to spend time with many different Christian denominations and try to understand their differences. Mostly I find it to be lot of very silly stuff. I know they do not think it's silly stuff. That's life in the big city.

However, I had been raised as a good Catholic boy, and I had no problem with Ann joining the Catholic Church. It was unusual to find someone choosing to be a Catholic, as many of those raised Catholic tend to let it drop as they get older. My brothers and sister were all quite impressed, and they came over for the confirmation ceremony, and we had a great meal together afterwards.

Raising the roof

In the early nineties, we thought about expanding the size of our small two-bedroom house. To help us with this project, we had a friend by the name of Allen Smith, an architect by trade and a great builder, who visited us in Peach Bottom. He had the thought that we could remove the roof and put a second floor on the house, which would double the square footage of the house and give two extra sizeable bedrooms, a large bathroom with a door from each bedroom, plus a walk-in closet and a high outside deck from the bigger of the two bedrooms. To do all this we would need a house improvement bank loan.

While this was all happening, Ann was still in the middle of pursuing her law degree, which was very time-consuming for her. I felt that myself and Allen working together could handle it. No way did I think I could do a good job by myself. Allen had himself a very unique B and B right in the middle of a town. He had taken a big old house and converted it into a beautiful building with five or six large bedrooms, each with its own theme and fireplace. It was a very nice piece of work he put together. So I was honored to be able to work with him on our home in Peach Bottom.

What Allen asked us to do was give him all the inside wall-to-wall measurements of all the existing rooms. Allen took those measurements and drew up the plans. When he gave me the plans, I talked to a building-supply business close by. They sent a representative over to look at the plan and the house that the plans were intended for. He came back a few days later with a long list of supplies that would be needed.

Now it went back to Allen, who had people that he worked with before, who could do the removal of the present roof and build the knee wall extension and complete the new roof work. This was an Old Order Mennonite family that had their own crew, a father and three sons. The Old Order Mennonites lived almost the same life style as the Amish. One thing that I noticed was they had bicycles, and the Amish were not allowed to use bicycles. When I asked the Amish what was the thinking behind that, I was told that they did not want to risk the Amish wanting to also ride motor cycles.

The crew lived over an hour's drive away, and they did not drive or own motor vehicles. As I had four workers to pick up every work day, my little S-10 pickup would not be big enough. I was lucky enough to have a nice 1964 Cadillac Coupe DeVille. The father sat in the front seat and the three sons sat in the back seat. They all wore their large black hats that covered the area from window to window in the back seat. The Cadillac was a head turner in itself. People would take a double take when they saw who my passengers were.

They had to have a window of time to get the job done, as the weather is always a concern when you are removing a roof, and completely building a second floor. I had the supplies delivered and covered with a tarp. Allen made the call as to when to start, in the hope that we could remove and replace the whole of the roof without weather-related problems.

After Allen made the call to start the project, I would leave the house at 6 am, pick the workers up at 7 am, and they would work from 8 am thru to 6 pm each day. Things were going well weatherwise until a few days into the job. It was about mid-day when it looked like thunderstorm clouds were building on the horizon and starting to close in. It was late in the day and they worked right up to darkness, and the roof was still not completely done. My neighbors saw I was in trouble and came over to see if they could help. We gathered up all the tarps we could find and all the lines and ropes we could pull together. They came over and parked their vehicles and turned on the headlights. There must have been eight of us. We did get it all secured, and then took a deep breath and hoped it did not get blown off by the wind. It was not long before the sky opened up and it poured down. The tarps stayed on, and inside, the house stayed dry. Another three days and the roof was secured.

Now to put the other pieces together. I had some young Amish workers who could do the carpentry work. They were fun to work with, as they were still young and not yet fully integrated into the Amish order. They liked working away from other church members. I used to drive to their homes and pick them up. On the way to the job they would ask me to go by a wooded area, and they would go off and pick up a ghetto-blaster for some music, which was a no-no to all members. Then when I would bring them home, I would drive by the wooded area and they would hide their music box.

One Saturday I was watching some thoroughbred horse racing on the television, and they were upstairs working away, and I asked them down and explained how, if they wanted to, they could make a bet on any horse they wanted, and could win some money as I would take their bet. I paid them at the end of each day they worked, so they had money. I still do not know for sure if betting is unacceptable in the Amish church. I tried to explain to them how the odds on each horse were different, and how much money they could win betting on different horses. They thought about it for a while and decided they did not want to bet and maybe lose some of their hard-earned money.

I also had the electrician working that same Saturday. He had bigger jobs that he worked during the week, and gave me a day of work on Saturday to help a neighbor and earn some extra money. He was not Amish and was a bit older. He thought it was interesting to see me trying to tempt these two young Amish lads into making some easy money. The Amish lad, Elmer, who was the main carpenter, asked me if I wanted to buy a generator for his family, and he would rent it off me. I asked why his family wanted to rent the generator, and his answer was the bishop did not allow members to own a generator, but they could rent one. I just felt I did not want to get into the craziness and declined. We got quite friendly with the carpenter's father and his family.

After the Old Order Mennonites had finished their work, I had very little need of Allen, as now I was pretty much the general, lining up the other sub-contractors. My next door neighbor was a big help. I picked up some nice wood from a friend for all the trim work inside, and my neighbor cut this out on his own saw. He also helped me out when I got hold of a long straight poplar tree. I always had some good wedges for splitting logs. Together we split the long log into four long supports for the sun deck coming out from the new bedroom.

I was also very lucky to find a very old indoor maple floor, that was salvaged from a building that was ruined. It was pretty dirty, as it had been sitting for a long time. It took a lot of sanding to get it all down to bare wood so I could put a few coats of varnish on it. It really came up nice. Those rough-cut poplar pillars to hold up the deck, plus all the nice trim and hardwood floors added a lot to the value of the whole job. We moved up to our new large bedroom, bathroom and walk-in closet the summer of 1992. We did not live there much longer though, as things changed and in late December,1993 we moved from Peach Bottom to Lancaster, after seven years at Peach Bottom.

Move to Lancaster

Ann had been working in Lancaster for those seven years, and once she finished her law degree and passed the Bar exam, she was starting to build an immigration law practice of her own in Lancaster, which had a medium size Hispanic population as a base to cultivate. This moved along swiftly, and she eventually had her own building and was running the only immigration law practice in Lancaster. She now thought that, as she was opening her own office in Lancaster, it would be better to live there, and I had no problem with that, being the adventurer I am. It had been a long time since I lived in a city though.

Raising the Roof

House before renovation, 1986

Halfway through...

Securing open gables before storm

House after renovation 1992

We put the house up for sale and started looking in Lancaster for another house. I always enjoyed looking to buy, more than looking to sell, but we found a buyer pretty quick for Peach Bottom. The agent for the buyer was trying to get financing, which went on for a while and never did get approved. We were lucky as we got a second buyer pretty quickly, with no problem getting the financing. We were looking all around Lancaster for something that would suit our needs.

Ann finally found a house that caught her fancy. It was centrally located and within walking distance for work. It was an older city home with three floors, with a separate bath and small kitchen on the third floor. The house had been on the market for a long time. The house had been completely upgraded by the present owner - all new windows, electrics, plumbing, and she had spent a lot of money on it, probably more than the house was worth. I do not think she was too happy with the cost of the whole project. She very much wanted to sell the house, as she offered the broker extra commission to get a buyer. The sale went through and we made the move, the day after the closing of the sale in Peach Bottom. I still had my 64 Cadillac, with no garage in Lancaster for the 'pride and joy'. I parked it outside behind a friend's house. It was hard, parking the car outside in the middle of winter, with all the bad weather.

We came out of the sale with a few dollars profit. I was looking for a garage and found two that were for sale right close to the house. The lot also had a nice piece of land behind it, maybe forty feet by twenty feet. It took a little time, but we got a loan from Ann's brother and a deal with the owner. Now I had two garages with income for one and one for myself. I also had a nice place to run a garden in the city. A bit of Irish luck, as it is not easy to find shelter for your 'pride and joy' but also someplace to grow vegetables in the center of a city.

Life in the City

It did not take me long to re-learn a few city life realities. For example, after the first snowfall with enough accumulation, it was clear that a shovel would be needed. There was not too much area to be cleared of snow. I went out and shoveled the area so people could walk with less fear of a slip. The snow shovel was wet and I laid it against the outside wall to dry, then went inside for a cup of tea or something. That is something country folk do all the time, as nobody wants to carry wet tools inside a dry house. I was not in there long. When I came out again, the shovel must have grown wings as it was gone ! I looked around and did not see anybody to ask if they had seen anyone take my shovel.

When the thief came walking by I am sure he did the same thing - looked around, did not see anybody, picked up my shovel and walked on around the corner and disappeared into the maze of the big city. That was a good wake-up call to remind me of city living.

There was another lesson to be learned. I was doing a lot of golfing during this period and I used to leave my golf clubs in the garage. I always left the garage door open when I was working in the garden behind it. The next time I went looking for my golf bag, it also disappeared. Thieves can be pretty bold - he or she must have seen the door open and the golf clubs inside. Looked around and did not see anybody, picked up the golf clubs, put them over their shoulders and walked away into infinity. Lesson number two. When I was involved in the boxing club down in Costa Rica, I used to tell the boxers in the club, 'You will get hit with some punches, but (I like to use the word 'but' sometimes) if you get hit by the same punch twice, you are doing something wrong'. I should listen to myself more often !

I still very much enjoyed city living as every thing is close. Supermarkets, department stores and many other shops. Lancaster also had a nice little live theater, nice entertainment and support for the art itself.

Another Costa Rica trip

I had had very good luck with the S-10 Chevy pick-up I bought in the mid-eighties, that had 197,000 miles on the clock with no major problems. I decided that I would drive it down to Costa Rica, sell it down there and fly back and get the new truck. I also had a 1964 Cadillac Deville that I had for years, that I also had to try and find a good home for somewhere else.

So that was the plan, and I decided to drive south-west down to the Texas-Mexico border and make the crossing right south of Corpus Christi, Texas. Then drive down the Gulf coast side of Mexico as far as the shortest crossing over to the Pacific side, to proceed through all the central American countries to Costa Rica.

I always enjoyed the solitude of long drives. I packed the truck with what I wanted to take down there with me. The first stop I made was West Virginia to see a close friend who I knew years ago when we both lived in Costa Rica, and he had a farm down there with a caretaker living there. He asked me to bring some things down for his farm caretaker, whom I knew well. I stayed there with him and his family for a few days and got some minor work done on my windshield wipers which I knew I would need.

After I left West Virginia, I headed south west to Louisiana and crossed over to Texas and south along the Gulf of Mexico till I got to the border. It took about three days. I was also given a stray dog in West Virginia that was not used to traveling in a car and got sick in the cab a couple of times before he got used to it. It was a real mess to clear up. When I got to the border, I felt it would be best for the dog and me to leave him at a shelter and see if they could find a good home for him. I found an animal shelter where there was a chain and a peg in the ground that I hooked him onto.

The next day I tried to cross the border and was turned away as I had four spare tires in the bed, and I was only allowed one. It was a bummer. On the way back to where I stayed the night before, I stopped by the dog shelter to see how the dog was sorted. I talked to the operator and told him the story about my crossing problems. He gave me the number of a coyote who could get me across. I called and we agreed on a price. The next morning we got together and started driving west along the border. We drove for about two hours to the next border crossing and went right through - nothing about the extra tires in the back. I then drove back along the other side of the border back to the crossing where I was turned back. He got paid and I headed south along the coast.

I got about 30 miles south and there was another checkpoint. I think they only had two guards there so they came out of their little office and saw the tires in the truck-bed and said I had to go back to the border. After what I just went through, I said I was not going back to the border. I asked who was the patron (boss), it was the older of the two; I asked if we could go into the office and talk. So here we are in the office, and I just asked how much plata (money) he wanted. He said 40 dollars and I said I will give you 20, and a second or two went by and he said OK. I gave him the 20 dollars and went on down the road. I was thinking is this going to happen everytime for whatever reason I am pulled over or have to go through a border? I put it on the back burner and continued down the road.

I was now feeling pretty good as I was well into a part of Mexico that was new to me. When I started to feel like I needed something in my stomach, I would start to look for a place that looked OK. In the late afternoon, I would start to think about where I wanted night to catch me. I would scan anyplace that looked like they had a bit of security and pull in and check it out. I would always be up at first light to get on the road. It was great to see the sun come up over the Gulf of Mexico, which happened every day as the weather was good.

The first thing I would look for is someplace where I could get some coffee. As the morning progresses you can see how the shops all start to open. Usually the first one to open served coffee. I would wait for a couple more hours to work up an appetite for a big breakfast and more coffee. On a full day of chasing the white line, I would be able to get between 5 and 7 hundred miles behind me. The southern part of Mexico is not too well populated, so the towns and villages are pretty far apart. The downside of the S-10 hevy I was driving was it had a small gas tank. I was very conscious of where the gas needle was all the time. If it got below half I was looking for someplace to fill it up again.

So on the second day, I was close to Valparaiso which is Mexico's biggest port on the Gulf side of Mexico. They export a lot of citrus from there, plus other fruits. The Gulf side of Mexico is much more fertile than the Pacific side, which is like a desert in the dry season. I much prefer the Gulf side as it is much greener all year around. As I was driving through Valparaiso I must have made a wrong turn and was pulled over by a guard. I showed him my papers and then asked how much is the multa (fine) for whatever I was supposed to have done which caught his attention. It was not cheap, but if you push it up to the next level of authority, it could be a lot more money and time. I paid it, and was glad to be back on the road. I was now looking for the road to make the crossing to the Pacific side for the rest of the trip south. I found the road, and you could see the big changes in the land - whatever was growing was getting browner and browner as you got closer to the Pacific. So from here on south this is what it will be like as far as you want to go. So after three nights in Mexico, I was at the Guatemala border.

Right at the border there was a bit of delay, and I made it into a restaurant to get a bite to eat. The place was busy so I asked a couple if I could join their table. They were an American couple heading north, so as I was heading south, I asked what could I expect on the road south. I told them what my destination was, and they asked me if I had a map, which I did not. I think they thought that was a bit strange, as they had a whole book of maps. I just knew I wanted to stay on Route One. That was the main road all the way through to where I wanted to go. Well, they thought I should have a map. So what they did was tear a piece out of their book, that showed Route 1 going all the way to Costa Rica. I kept it with me all the way down, and I did look at it when I was not sure.

With the delay, it was not possible to make it through Guatemala in one day. I did get through without any major problems, as all my papers were in order and nothing came up on the tires, so that was good. I got a good way into Guatemala before I had to find someplace to pass the night. The place I found was alright but I think it was a heart-shape bed with mirrors all over the place. At the time it was getting late in the afternoon, and I did not want to end up sleeping in the truck on the side of the road. It is dangerous driving at night on the roads through there, as there are animals out on the roads that can cause problems if you hit one of those creatures. I made it pretty close to the El Salvador border. I left my strange room at first light and made it down to the border early Sunday morning. The border was very quiet and I passed out of Guatemala quite quickly.

Getting into El Salvador was something else. The one fellow I was talking to there lost a leg above the knee and had a false leg. That was when El Salvador was in the middle of a civil war, and he was a victim of that long war. He told me he went up to the US to get his false leg and he had a lot of appreciation for what the USA did for him. As an

American traveling through these countries, that appreciation makes you feel much more comfortable.

So we were there for a while waiting for someone who had a stamp to show up, but nothing. So he went off with my passport and papers, and came back with all the necessary stamps. He told me he had to wake the boss up so he could give me the stamps I needed to get into and out of El Salvador. It was a pleasant border crossing. I gave him a handsome tip.

I then had a full day of not too much traffic but some poor roads, which will happen when a country is in a long civil war. There was one point where I was not even sure I was still on Route One. I was driving through this little village and stopped for a bite to eat. I talked to these fellows and asked if this was Route 1. They said it was, and that it's the best road they have. It was really a bad stretch of the Central American main road.

I was moving along at a steady pace, thinking I might be able to get into Honduras before night caught me. So I was getting close to the border and moving at a good speed when I got pulled over a few miles from the border. It was two guards, one young one and one older one. I was talking to the older one - the road only went to one place, so he knew I was on my way out. So then the young one told me something about a zipper. I had no idea what he was talking about so I looked at him and repeated the word. Then he showed me how the seat belt goes on. So that was his word for seat belt. He told me he wanted some plata (money), so, having a few notes of local money, I reached into my pocket and threw them out the window. I then just drove off, heading to the border.

When I got down to the border there were hundreds of people there. They told me the border was closed until six o'clock the next morning. People started jumping on the truck bumpers and I knew I did not want to spend the night there. I got the truck turned around and they all jumped off, as they knew I was going to leave. While driving up the road I remembered a place I had seen that looked pretty secure, not far up the road. I also knew I had to drive past the two guards that stopped me coming the other way. I was not going to stop on the way back and I think they knew that. They also must have known the border was closed for the night, but they did not tell me. When I was getting close to their check point, I started speeding up, and I saw them sitting on the porch of the house right off the road. They waved to me, and I just beeped the horn and kept on going. I found the place I was looking for and it was comfortable and secure. I had a good night's sleep, and at first light I was back on the road to the border again. I did not see the two guards that stopped me the day before.

When I got to the border this time it was much better. So I got some coffee and got in line. The line was still pretty long and I was waiting, and I finally got a chance to talk to someone, and he was not a nice man. For all my stamps I would need a hundred dollars. Now that was high and he also knew it. He was not going to come down any. I just looked at him, and he knew I was mad. He was not going to move and wanted to keep working, so I gave it to him. I knew before I left that I would be easy pickings for greedy people who work at borders as I have crossed quite a few borders through the years. He got me, but I got into Nicaragua with no problems.

I was not too far into Nicaragua when there were two ladies looking for a lift. I had been traveling alone for a while and they looked alright, so I gave them a lift. I did not have the radio on the whole way down, and when they saw the radio, they sure wanted to turn that radio on. I asked how far they were going, and they said the capital Managua. That was the one city that, looking at my little map, I had no way to avoid driving through. I told them where I was going and asked if there was any way I could avoid driving through the capital. They said they would put me on a road that would take me right down to the border. I thought that it may be better to listen to them, than getting lost in a dangerous big city. We kept on driving, I kept following the signs for the capital. I was thinking we were getting awful close, and then they said to make a turn onto another road. I made the turn and they said that is where they wanted to get off. They told me just stay on that road, and it would take me right to the border. I went driving down the road, drove quite a bit and still no signs. I was just hoping that I was heading if not on the right road at least in the right direction. Then a big sign popped up, and it showed the name (which I now forgot) of the border crossing town. I took a deep breath, as it was a sign that I had really been wanting to see. That was to be my last border crossing for a while.

When I got to the border it was late afternoon, and I got through with no trouble. The border guard did ask me about the tires though. I said I did not want to talk about the tires, and he said no more. It was great to be back in CR. The roads in Costa Rica are much better than the rest of Central America. Their whole infrastructure had benefited after the war of 1948, from their decision to abolish their army, which made money available for spending on health and education. Also, Costa Rica had been into promoting tourism since the early seventies, that brought a lot of money into the country and they did not have any wars. That gave Costa Rica a big jump economically on the rest of the Central American countries. It was the only country where I drove on the road at night since I left Texas.

The first stop I had planned was with my long time friend, Gene Sanders, who I got to know in Cahuita not long after I first arrived down there. He was a pilot for another American that he was down there with. He kept the plane down in Puerto Viejo where there was a small grass air strip. I made some trips with him to San Jose and back to the bush. I now found a place to spend the night and get some sleep.

He was living in Puntarenas, which is the biggest port on the Pacific side of the country. I had no problem finding him, and the first words out of his mouth I will never forget. He said to me, I was like a breath of fresh air. To me that was a great welcome. He had another friend with him that he knew for years and I had met before. He was a fellow pilot from time gone by. He was now well into Costa Rica life, with a Tico wife and kids. The wife and the younger kids were living in Limon where her sister also lived. He was over in Puntarenas with his son, taking tourists out on day sport fishing trips. He was full into catch and release fishing. He was the only sport fisherman with a sport fishing boat that never had a fish in it.

As you can imagine my truck was pretty dirty after weeks on the road without a cleaning. His son did a great job cleaning the truck. He took the seat covers off and washed them in the machine and cleaned the truck like I had not seen it for awhile. Gene told me he had a paid job, taking full charge of the Yacht Club there, which had a lot of traffic moving north and south. They also had some yachts that had Costa Rica flags, it was their home port. With his background and knowledge, he was well suited for the job.

    I spent maybe a week down there with Gene, then decided to make my way back up to the capital to see Albert, my sailboat friend from Cahuita, who was now building 30- and 40-foot outstanding sport fishing boats, which became well known in the sport fishing world for the right reasons. I still had my four tires and all the stuff that David put in there for his caretaker over in Cahuita. So I thought it was time to lighten up my load. I also let it be known that my truck was for sale. I dropped off the extra tires in Limon, with a good friend who was good at selling stuff. I left the tires with him and he found a buyer, and I got 200 dollars for the tires and rims. It would have been much better if I had left them in Lancaster with the little financial return and all the aggro they had caused.

    Two days in San Jose was enough - I went back down to the bush. This was the first time back when I did not have my own place. I went up the north beach and stayed with Taxi-Cab Steve. I knew him from back in the seventies, when he would spend three months a year down there from right after the New Year till sometime in March. He was up there by himself, so he enjoyed the company and I had transportation, where he just had his little motorized scooter. His farm bordered David's, and I had a lot of stuff for his caretaker. When I got up there, I sent a message over to him that I had some good stuff for him from David. He came over and when I showed him what I had, it made for a good day for him and his lady friend.

    I thought about maybe trying to get a little softball tournament going. Maybe six teams with each having a home and away game. I moved up and down the coast to see how many players the settlements still had available. It was a major time of transition, with people getting out of agriculture and into tourism. I found a lot of the previous players were just too busy to put the time in for a few practices and the games themselves. I was never able to put it together with the changing times. Anyway, I really was not going to be down there long enough to do any really serious sport promotions.

I went back up to San Jose and found I had someone who might be interested in the truck. He had opened up a high-class fishing camp on an island that was not easy to get to. He invited me down to do some fishing which I accepted, and it was not easy. It was a long drive, and then you had a half-day to get out to the island. He had put a really nice fish camp together, with nice cabins and first class service and food. He also had arranged that you could fly in with a sea-plane he had on call. He did get some high-roller clients. He never did buy my truck though. But I had a solid buyer for the truck down in Puntarenas, so I went down and sold the truck, bought a plane ticket back to Harrisburg, Pennsylvania, and was home in a few days.

CHAPTER 4 - BACK TO IRELAND AND MORE TRAVELS

End of our marriage

However, over our six years in Lancaster, our relationship became more unstable and was heading towards the rocks. Neither of us was happy with the way things were going for perhaps many reasons. Ann knew that I did not want to continue to live in Lancaster. Anyhow, I was open to a move.

It was late in the summer of '99 that I made a trip over to Ireland to visit family and friends, which turned out to be a life-changing one for me. I stopped up to Donegal to visit my aunt Annie, who was my last surviving relative in Ireland. Annie gave me a choice – she offered me an empty house that had belonged to my uncle Joe, perhaps 15 miles from hers. I asked about the old homestead in Upper Carrigart, as I said I would rather be closer to the sea. I would also be closer to her. So she said I could have the key to the old homestead. The house had been empty for about 6 years since my uncle Barney passed away in February 1993, and this was 99. I told her I would be back in a few months, after I got things sorted out in the USA. So I made one brief trip back to Lancaster after I got the key in the fall of 1999, returned to Donegal in November, and one trip back after I finished the house renovation project, in March 2000. That first trip was when I arranged to take my white 90 Cadillac 2-door Coupe Deville across, something I did not want to leave behind.

It was a great opportunity and a project that I would enjoy. I booked my ticket back for November 1999, and sorted out transportation of my 'pride and joy' by ship out of Baltimore, Maryland to Amsterdam, Holland. I made arrangements to drop the car off at the dock in Baltimore for shipping. It worked out well, as my sister Helen's son Eddie drove out to Lancaster, where I put my bags in his car, then I drove the Cadillac to Baltimore to drop off at the dock for shipment. I arranged to meet up with him at the dock with him picking me up and driving me on to the Baltimore airport for my plane trip to Ireland. It was due to arrive in Amsterdam, Holland, in a few weeks. So, from

November 1999 to March 2000, I was working on the reconstruction of the old house.

When I got back to Lancaster in spring of 2000, it took a while to sort things out as to my worldly possessions - what to sell, what to leave and see if someone else wanted to sort it out. The big thing was what to take with me. The house in Lancaster was to be rented out to the family of one of Ann's colleagues, she had decided to move back to Belfast, Northern Ireland, to stay with an ecumenical religious community. She did not want to stay in the States alone. There were items in the house that I could also use over in Ireland. I had a great handyman whose services I had used for years – so I got him to build a box for shipping over to Ireland. It was about three feet x three feet x six feet. We packed a corner cabinet made by the Amish, that took up a lot of the space, and along with that, a lot of hard-to-find stuff and tools.

Aunt Maggie's trunk

At a later stage, I also shipped the old trunk that my aunt Maggie kept in her basement for many years. It was the same trunk that my grandmother had packed with all the things she thought she would need for the ship's crossing from Scotland to America. It is one of a kind, as it was a custom-built by a local craftsman, who built the truck with a small tray fitted across half the inside top, to keep the smaller stuff for easy access.

My aunt Maggie told me that she had a lock of my mother's hair that she brought over in the trunk – she did not tell me why. When I got the trunk, it was complete, but some wood had to be replaced and the whole trunk had to be sanded down to the bare wood and varnished. I found a key to fit the lock, so it was a complete trunk again.

I am now eighty years old. It was in the late twenties when my maternal grandfather came over first with the older boys, Willie and Eddie, and some of the older girls. After I completed the job, I gave it back to her and she had it in her living-room as a nice offee table. She enjoyed it for a year or two before she peacefully passed away. Her son brought it back to me, as she wanted me to have it. It was very nice of him and his mother. I have it in my bedroom now, so I see it and enjoy it everyday. It was good the day it was made, and served its purpose as a super large suitcase for my grandmother and her young children for a transatlantic ship's crossing. It looked bad the day she showed it to me and asked if I wanted to do something with it. I enjoyed bringing it back to a beautiful piece of work, after perhaps fifty years in a cold damp basement, and I still enjoy it today. I keep it as a night table for my bed and useful for some extra storage space.

So after packing up my stuff and shipping it out, and having booked a flight in September 2000 to Shannon, I picked up a rental car in Ireland until I could buy one to use over there. My city life had just ended, after 7 years. It was the beginning of my new life in Donegal, Ireland. The house in Lancaster was eventually sold a couple of years later.

Renovating the old homestead

When I got back in November 1999, I moved in with my dear old Aunt Annie who was 83 years old and was living in an old people's council cottage down the road from the old homestead. The council houses were built down there in the late seventies, so she would have been in her mid sixties when she moved into her brand new council house. It had a range in the living room and a small kitchen off to the back with one bedroom. She gave me some blankets, and the couch was my new bed until I got the old house to a point where I could move in. The place was warm and comfortable, especially around dinner time with the range being fired up to cook the dinner. She cooked a boiled egg for me every morning and a dinner every evening. She told me she was not going to wash my clothes. I am sure she would have taken on the job of washing my clothes if she had had a washing machine, which she did not have and had never had. I did not have many clothes, so I sorted it out without any problem. I was well used to being in small spaces with few belongings from my time on merchant ships.

It was the beginning of a great relationship. I had got to know her a bit from my time living in County Clare and making trips up for visits, but this was different. After I moved into the old house, I would stop down to see her every day about 3 pm, to have a cup of tea with a scone or cake and to let her know how the project was moving along.

I also took over from Willie the mission of taking her for doctors' appointments and shopping whenever necessary. She had never had the opportunity to meet my brothers Eddie or Joe, and my brother John and sister Helen only once. She really did not even know my father, as he left for America when she was six. I in return did not know her or her four brothers, whom I had never met before I made my first visit to Ireland in the mid seventies. At that time she was still living in the old homestead with her brother Barney.

It was in the late seventies or early eighties that they built the old people's cottages that she was now living in. She had the offer of one of the cottages. She had to make a decision whether to take it or not. She had lived her whole life in the old family home. As it turned out she took the house offered by the council. For the first time in her sixty plus years of life, she had inside water, a bathtub and flush toilet, which I am sure she enjoyed. Now it was my home also for the next three plus months.

Fetching the 'pride and joy'

I was not too far into the project when I got word my 90 Cadillac arrived in Amsterdam, Holland. I had to make a trip over to pick it up and drive it back to Ireland. There was a bus that left Letterkenny at 8am. It went from Letterkenny to Belfast, where we boarded the ferry for the short crossing of the Irish sea to Scotland. In Scotland I boarded another bus to the main train station in Glasgow, Scotland. There was a great train service from Glasgow to Edinburgh, a very modern and fast train. The trip took two hours. As it was starting to get late, I decided to pass the night in Edinburgh. As my mother was born and raised in Bathgate not far south of Edinburgh, I used to hear a lot about how good the shopping was on Princes street. I checked the times for trains departing for Newcastle, England and then booked a hotel on Princes street not far from the train station. The next day I would be back at the train station for my trip to Newcastle, England, and a taxi to the port to board the overnight ferry to Amsterdam, Holland.

While in Edinburgh I called my brother Joseph to let him know where I was, as I am sure he heard more about Princes Street than I did. We had a good chat as I told him what my mission was on this trip. The next day I went back to the train station and bought my ticket to

Newcastle. The train was not as modern or as fast as the Glasgow – Edinburgh train. It did not make any difference as I had all day to get to the ferry port to purchase my passage and cabin for the overnight trip to Amesterdam. When I got to the port terninal I still had a few hours before sailing. I had no problem getting a berth for the night.

I arrived in Amsterdam well-rested and found a nice little family hotel. I told the owners what I had to do and that I needed a parking place for the car. They were very helpful and found a place for the car. I had never done this before, so I had no way of knowing how long it would take and what I needed to get the car from Customs. I did not think I would have any problems booking my passage back to Newcastle. I got the car the next day from Customs after I bought two weeks' worth of car insurance to drive the car back to Ireland. I got back to the hotel and parked the car with no problems.

Now I had to make reservations for my passage back over to England and from Scotland to Ireland. To my surprise they were all booked for the next few days, as this was getting close to Christmas and a lot of people were traveling. I asked the agent if there was another way I could go. I was told there was a ferry that ran from Rotterdam to Hull, England. I booked the Rotterdam crossing, but was told all the cabins were sold out for the overnight crossing. Then I knew it was going to be a long night. The drive from Amsterdam to Rotterdam was a pleasant trip, I was not pushed for time as the ship did not leave until early evening. I boarded the ship and found my seat which was like something you would find on a bus. As the night went on, I could not sleep in that very uncomfortable chair. I decided to lay down on the deck, which was cold hard steel. I could at least stretch out, so I did get a very little sleep. The ship arrived in Hull at 7am. After clearing customs and immigration, it was 8 am when I hit the road for Stranraer, Scotland.

I had a map of England and Scotland and I knew I had to cross England and head north to Scotland. The thing I found out about crossing the Midlands of England is that there are a lot of lakes. That makes it very hard to keep your bearing as to north, south, east or west, with an overcast sky and a cold rain.on top of that. I had to pull off the road a few times to take another look at the map, and I also had to get used to driving on the left hand side of the road, with the steering wheel also on the left side.

I finally got on the west of England motorway heading horth towards Scotland. I looked at my map when I got up to Scotland, and I had to make a choice, as there were two roads to take. Go around the coast road or the high road. It was early to mid afternoon, it was raining and the temperature was close to freezing. If I went high, it was possible to run into some snow cover on the road. That could also happen on the low road but less likely. It was a really nice drive in a nice riding car. It was about a two-hour ride to the ferry terminal and the ferry was scheduled to leave at 4 pm. I pushed along, and time-wise it was close as I pulled up to the entrance to the ferry - there were no vehicles there and I could see the ferry. I showed my papers and was told to drive to the ferry. There were crewmen there who directed me where to park. I was the last one on the ferry. There were very few cars on there, mostly all lorries. I parked and went up to the top deck where I could smell the food. They had a really nice layout and I was super-tired and just as hungry. I had a good feed and found a place to lay my head. I do not think my head was down but for a few minutes and I was in a deep sleep. The next thing I heard over the loudspeaker was 'return to your vehicle'.

I talked to another driver and asked for directions to a pub in Belfast where I had never been before. He gave me good directions as it was on the south side of Belfast. The ferry dock was well north of Belfast, so it was about a hour's drive. It was a well-known pub in Belfast and the local pub of my friend, Gerry, which was the only info I had on him. I found the pub and went in and talked to the barman - he knew my friend and gave me an address and told me how to get there. I found the house and knocked on the door - he did not have a telephone, so I could not let him know I was in Belfast. A woman answered the door and she did not know me, so I asked if I could talk to Gerry. She turned around and called Gerry, and told him somebody was here looking for him. He came to the door and saw me and it was a bit of a suprise, as I had not seen or communicated with him for as many as ten years. So we had our

Cadillac

1964 Cadillac Fleetwood with only 50,000 miles on the clock

First place trophy at the All-American Car Show, Kilbeggan, Co. Westmeath, Ireland 2005

hellos and the pat on the back. When we walked in, the woman, whose name I still did not know, said to me 'he was sure glad to see you'. That was a nice welcome. I was just glad that I did not have to look for a place to pass the night. Gerry had a bottle of cider he was drinking, and me and his partner had tea. We talked well into the night.

I asked Gerry if he could put me on the Derry road in the morning, as it was in North Belfast and it would make it easier for me to have somebody who knew where he was going. He told me he had to walk a dog for a neighbor, and asked if he could bring the dog with him. No problem, just put me on that Derry road, so I can find my way home with my 'pride and joy'. Finally, I pulled into my parking spot in the council house lot and parked my 'pride and joy'.

I could have made arrangements to have the car shipped door to door. Picked up in Lancaster, PA. USA and dropped off in Carrigart, Ireland. It would have cost a lot more money, but even more important I would not have this story to tell !

I also picked up a Volvo Estate (station wagon), a very heavy sturdy machine that I would use as a work-horse while gutting and rebuilding the old house. Later I sold my 90 Cadillac Fleetwood to the same gentleman who sold me the Volvo, who got many years of enjoyment with the Cadillac.

Fixing up the old homestead

To help me with work on the reconstruction project, I had one very knowledgeable man who spent years in the building trade. He was a friend of my late uncle Barney and ran errands for my Aunt Annie. My next door neighbor who had a small farm also helped. As there had been no vehicles down there for years, the road was impassable and needed a lot of work. My neighbor had a large Cat digger that he used, to supplement his farm income, and I needed his help to open the road. I dumped a lot of stone to firm the road up for what was coming. Meantime me and Willie, my main man, who could do almost any construction work, gutted the house - and we ended up with a big pile of clean waste; so my neighbor not only did the road work, he dug a deep hole for waste, and we also burnt some.

The floor in one room was wood and rotted out, so that was pulled up and six inches of cement was poured, with cross beams, and a new wooden floor was put in. All the plaster was taken off the four-hundred-year-old stone walls, that were three feet thick. The house was built before cement was invented, so it was a dirty job. We got one extra man for help. I had to design a living space that would be comfortable in a small space. The house never had inside water before and it had very basic electricity. I also had to get new piping to bring water down to the house. The house had been empty for six years and during that time they had put a new water main along the road (but on the other side of the road) that I had to tap into and bring across the road and down to the house. I also was going to put in an oil heater, and the road down to the house was not capable of handling an oil delivery truck, so I had to put the oil tank close to the top of the road. Plus I was going to put a phone in the house, which it never had before. With the help of the digger, a two foot deep trench was dug, to take the heating, oil, water and telephone lines from the road to the house. Welcome to the 21st century!

I was the one who went to the building supply yard every morning to pick up whatever the workers needed for that day. The building supply yard.was located in Milford, about a fifteen mile trip. The owner was a young fellow who had just opened his own building supply yard after working many years in a bigger yard in Letterkenny. He gave me a line of credit of 10 thousand euros, which was very generous of him, as he did not know me at all. Every month he sent me an itemized statement which I paid when due. He was my main source of supplies, but I also needed things like wood and other smaller things. That was good as I got to know my way around the area. It was an interesting time, meeting all the new people and doing business with them. It worked out good, and I was learning more about my new parish.

Willie, my main man on the job, found an electrician for me who I still use to this day. Willie did all the plumbing and installed the heater and hot water tank, plus a stove with a back boiler to heat the radiators also. I also had to reline the chimney for the stove, in which I burnt peat,coal and wood for all the cooking and a lot of the heating of the house. Everything went through the range for the hot water tank, radiators and cooking. It was pretty much the center point of my living room and kitchen. It did use a lot of fuel.

Willie found a good cabinet maker who did all my kitchen cabinets and the doors to the bedroom and bathroom. I had some very old beds made by a neighbor, which were a non-standard size, so I had to get some mattresses made to fit the measurements of the beds. The project was finally getting close to completion where I could move in. Annie was glad to get her place to herself and I was going to move out. The first night down there was the 17th of March 2000 (Saint Patrick's Day), it was like moving into a new house with a lot of family history.

Between Donegal and Belfast

So that's how I got to be in the house where we live as a family now. Returning to live again in Ireland after sixteen years living abroad was really a great experience, with all the positive changes. Those all started with the Good Friday peace agreement between the two communities, with the active support of US President Bill Clinton and the leader of Britain at the time, Tony Blair. Another important player was George Mitchell, who was present to assist all participants in the negotiations. It came to its conclusion on Good Friday of the year 1998. The agreement got the voting approval of all the people of nothern Ireland and the Republic of Ireland. When our family departed Ennistymon in 1983, the troubles were a part of everyday life in all of the island of Ireland since the mid-sixties, with death and destruction. With unemployment running high and a lot of migration on the upsurge, it was not a good time in Irish-English history, with no end in sight.

On my return in late ninety-nine, the whole mood of the country was upbeat, especially in Donegal, which is a border county. I talked to people who went shopping in the north for the first time in over 25 years, across an open border. Employment growth was happening, and a lot of the job-seekers who had migrated were returning to their home country. With the open border and help from both governments there were a lot of cross border business, social and sporting projects which are still active today.

Ann returned to Ireland in September 2000, and found an ecumenical community in north Belfast who offered her a position on a yearlong agreement. She also had a job with the local Legal Services Office providing immigration representation. I was spending my time between Donegal and Belfast as we were trying to keep our relationship going. My time in Donegal was spent on gardening and golf. I also spent an hour or so every day with my aunt having some good chats with tea and biscuits. I also made myself available for her shopping, doctor's appointments and any special events. The land had been neglected for the past few years as she lost interest. I got all the land ploughed and reseeded. The fences were repaired and drains cleared. Things were going well in Donegal.

Things in Belfast were quite different, but still interesting with the group all from different Christian communities living together in harmony as an example to the larger community, which was the main mission of the community. Those living in the group home included a Presbyterian minister from New Zealand and a retired Church of England clergyman.

One very interesting occasion was a visit by the Dalai Lama to Belfast, in support of peace and reconciliation of the Catholic and Protestant communities. He did a symbolic walk down a road that separated them, a small man in his Buddhist costume, dwarfed by all the media cameras and politicians walking with him. At the end of that walk, he mounted a makeshift stage and spoke about the need for peace.

During this time I also had a visit from my brother Joseph who spent three weeks with me. He was into his seventies, and this was his first trip to Ireland and his father's home. Annie was pleased to meet him for the first time, as she only knew about him from her brothers, Hughie and Mark, who knew him when he was very young when they were also living in Philadelphia.

I also had some friends from my time living in county Clare but now living in Belfast. It was great to be living in Ireland again and being of service to my aunt Annie. Ann and I also went on one or two trips together, one to the ecumenical Taize community in France, when we also went down to see her mother in southwest France. And another one to review various retreat centres in Scotland, which Ann had been asked to do for a friend of her mother's.

Ann's departure for France and Aunt Annie's death

After four years, as Ann's mother was becoming elderly and needed support, and it was clear that our paths were moving further and further apart, we agreed to informally separate, so she could move to live near her mother, and I would stay in Donegal. Ann left in September, 2004, and my life continued back in Donegal, without the weekly trip across the Glenshane Pass, which was a very nice drive with great views. Annie was getting close to ninety and still cooking her own potatoes which was great.

It wasn't until she turned 90 that she started to get complications with her health, and started to have blackouts. The first time, she was hospitalized with age-related problems for a week or so, to get treatment and get her strength back. She came back to her cottage and things went back to the way it was before. It was maybe four or five months later when she had another blackout and a fall. She went back to the Letterkenny hospital for treatment and got her strength back. She was in the hospital for a week or so, when she started to feel much better and wanted to go home. The first night back I spent the night down at her cottage. The next day we looked at the meds she had to take and when. This time she accepted the fact that she needed home help. The home help included coming to her cottage and cooking her a meal and cleaning the place. She was on a few drugs by this time and she wanted me to make sure she took the right drugs on time. I still got down to see her every day for tea and a long chat.

During this period another cottage became vacant and was completely done over. So it became like musical chairs. Her neighbor decided to move into the renovated cottage. His new cottage was completely renovated and Annie moved into a really nice newly renovated cottage. That was only her second move in over ninety years. Her first move was when she was over-sixty from the family homestead where I was now living, to a pensioner's cottage. Annie was into her sixties when she moved into the brand new pensioner's cottage down the road from the family homestead, and now at nearly ninety to a newly renovated cottage. She enjoyed this new cottage. It was a few months before the next medical episode happened and she was evaluated again and was told she would be taken to a nursing home. That is not what she wanted to hear, but she also knew I was not capable of doing what needed to be done. I made almost daily trips down to the nursing home, as she was not well in those surroundings. The nurse told me if she continued to regress they would send her back to the hospital. After spending years with her and with the last few months when her health deteriorated, I knew the hospital was not where she wanted to be. I passed my thoughts on to the nurse, and was told she would pass the message on to the doctor. I continued to see her everyday and not too long after, in the late evening, I got a call from the nursing home that she passed away peacefully in her sleep.

The next day I went to the nursing home and got her personal belongings, and proceeded to make arrangements for her church service and burial. I talked to the Parish priest and was told I would have to purchase a plot for two. The last plot the family had in the cemetery was full with the death years earlier of my Uncle Joe. Now I have a place in the long-term parking (cemetery), which I never thought much about before. The wake was held at her small cottage. The death was not announced on the local radio station, so the viewing did not draw a lot of people which was what she would want. All the local neighbors were there, her Doctor, Solicitor and her many local friends. Father Charley came by and the rosary was said by all. Me and a few neighbors and friends spent the night together, until the hearse came in the morning to take her to the same chapel where she was baptized, and had first communion and confirmation, for her requiem mass. The parish priest said a few nice words for one of the long-time members of his parish. After she was put to rest in the cemetery, a small group of maybe ten went to the Carrigart Hotel for a light meal.

I went back home to the ole homestead where my companion Finbarr was waiting for me, a wonderful loyal dog who came to me as a seven-week-old pup from one of Annie's neighbors from the council estate.

Annie had had a full life but also a very hard life, being the youngest daughter who watched three of her older brothers and her only sister migrate to Philadelphia, USA. The ones who were left at home were Annie, Joe and Barney. Their life on the small farm was bare subsistence farming and any help from the family over in America was very welcome, as it made their life better. Two of her brothers came back to Donegal and got their own farms. Annie being the only daughter still at home, took on the responsibility of caring for her elderly parents. Her father was the first to pass away, followed by her mother quite a few years later. The circumstance she was in now was the same as her brother Barney, who was also getting up in years, and she herself was getting up in years. Their chances of finding a partner under these circumstances were not very promising. When Annie moved into her pensioner's cottage she continued to care for and help Barney out with the farm. Before she offered me the keys to the old homestead, she was six years with no close family living in Ireland.

As for me, the keys to the house were a great gift. What was even greater than that was, I was able to spend time with this great lady who sacrificed her whole life for family and farm, so she was not alone. I truly believe I made the last six years of her tough life in the land of the living better, which I take comfort from. Her will was read and registered, but that is an interesting story for later. I knew I would miss those daily tea-and-biscuits chats.

An interlude of life on the ocean wave

The time after Annie's death I tried to keep busy, but it started to get a bit lonely down at the ole homestead with just me and Finbarr. Why do I keep moving? I was still active on my computer and I started to look for cruises. I was thinking about how it would be to spend the long winter nights in Donegal. I decided to make a trip over to visit family in the USA. A good website I found was called Vacations to Go, which sells a lot of cruises to a lot of places. I still recalled the trip me and Ann made from New York to Bermuda on a seven-day trip and how much I enjoyed being back at sea. I found that the best value based on cost per day is found when ships are relocating to a new home port or area like the Caribbean in the winter months, or to another area like Europe or Alaska for summer cruises. . . Eventually I found the relocation cruise of a Royal Caribbean ship Legend of the Seas from Europe in the fall to the Caribbean for the winter. It was a fourteen-day trip due to depart Southampton England Oct 21st, to arrive in Tampa, Florida on Nov 4th stopping at several islands in the Caribbean.

As I was planning on being gone for the winter I found a nice place for my best friend Finnbarr with my neighbor, who was good with dogs. I just had to drain all the water from the house to prevent freezing water pipes breaking causing major water damage. A direct flight from Dublin, Ireland to Southampton, England was booked plus a car rental in Tampa, Florida.

I boarded the ship and found my room, and I was really feeling good to be back on a ship for a trip from point A to B. I started finding my way around the ship and talking to other passengers. A majority of my fellow passengers were from Europe, mostly England. For most of my fellow passengers, this was not their first Transatlantic cruise. Some of the English passengers brought their own English tea bags with them for the trip over and for when they got to Florida. A lot of the other travelers had homes in Florida and planned it so they could winter there and return to England on perhaps the same ship in the spring, to spend the summer back in England until the ship is relocated again.

When we departed Southampton we headed south to the southern trade winds and the warmer weather. The shorter and faster crossing would be the northern crossing. But there is always the possibility that you could come in contact with an iceberg floating down from the Arctic, and the North Atlantic could get big waves that time of year. They have a saying if you want good weather follow the cruise ships.

It was a really great trip as I was lucky enough to find a good table for dinner, where there were the same passengers every night with excellent food and a good waiter from the Philippines. All the guests at our dinner table had some experience with the sea. One gentleman from Northern Ireland and his wife had done some lake sailing. Another gentleman and his wife from England was a retired big fishing boat captain who had some great stories. One was an attempted mutiny with drink involved, changing a cable on the lifeboat which he thought to be unsafe. I know from my time at sea it is a dirty nasty job, usually done in drydock in a shipyard by shipyard workers. Anoher time I saw a ship was delayed unloading, due to cables that the stevedores thought was unsafe. I have neve seen a cable burst apart, but from what I was told, it is dangerous if you are anywhere near. Mutiny is something all seamen think about, but I was never on a ship when it was attempted. The other couple was French who had very particular dietary needs, and these were well sorted by the cooks in the galley. They had a great command of the English language. The gentleman was someone who spent time on his own sailboat.

The last dinner at sea I asked the waiter if he wanted to tell us all about the place he came from in the Philippines. He was only too happy to let us all know more about him, the Philippines and how he found his way to sea. He and his wife both worked on the ship, and he had three children who were cared for by his mother in the Philippines.

When we docked in Tampa, there was an old restored Victory ship docked right behind us that was now a museum open to the public. It sure brought a smile to my face, as I spent many a day working on that class of ship and knew just how great a ship they were and the important part they played in our victory in the second world war.

Picked up my rental car at the airport and was on my way over to see my brother Joe, who had recently lost his wife of many years. I spent some time with him, and we planned a fourteen-day cruise to the southern Caribbean with Holland American lines on the Prinsendam, which is no longer in its fleet of ships. The reason I remember the ship so well is the hull design, which was a North Atlantic design for heavy seas, which is very rare for a cruise ship. The trip was over the Christmas and New Year holiday. It was a good trip where we had a good table for dinner with other long time cruisers. It was a good mix as we had two elderly gay men who were long time partners, a married couple, a single middle-aged woman and myself and Joe. Joe's physical condition was starting to deteriorate, and it was hard for him to get around the ship. He did try and get ashore in most ports. I think he missed one port. He did say if he made another trip he would get some medical work done on his legs.

As soon as we got back to Florida, I booked the first of four legs of a world cruise on the Holland American Amsterdam – starting with a passage through the Panama Canal, which I had not been through since the sixties. After passing through the Panama Canal, we headed south to Peru for an overnight stay. From there we headed across the big

South Pacific ocean, the first port of call being Easter Island, where back in the sixties in my merchant seaman days, I spent three months there with supplies for an air strip and very large sea buoys, for ships like this to make fast to while in port. I never really thought I would ever get back there. When I got ashore and started telling the islanders that I was there in the sixties with asphalt and tar to put in the air strip, it turned out most of them were not even born then. One young man I talked to said his grandfather told him stories about that time, as he had worked on the air strip. I also asked for directions to where I could find the priest Father Sebastian that I met down there and who gave me a wooden statue of the large stone heads. I was looking for his grave site. We found his grave and I said a prayer for his soul. From there we stopped at many more South Pacific islands. On this trip we also had a poker game every afternoon with no shortage of players.

What I found out about Holland American lines is that they catered especially for elderly guests, with great medical facilities on board the ship, as they even had kidney dialysis machines on board. The guests on this cruise were well-seasoned cruisers for the most part. On this 31-day leg of my world cruise, three guests passed away, one of the deceased being a poker player. When we learned that he passed away, the game stopped for a moment of prayer. The other two who passed away I did not know. I do believe the three who died were right where they wanted to be when the time came.

At the start of the trip, one of the crew asked me if I spoke another language, and I said I spoke a little Spanish. So, the first night they set the passengers to dinner tables they put me with a table of a large Mexican family as they thought I may fit well. The first night I tried, and it did not go well. The second night the Mexican family did not show up for dinner and I was there by myself at this large table, which was a bit embarrassing. Strange as it may sound, it worked out well, as the next night I was put with a really great table. For one couple, this was their first cruise and they wanted to go on a round-the-world cruise. All the others were well-seasoned cruisers. Except for me, they were all doing the entire 103-day trip. There was an elderly very nice woman who enjoyed playing the slot machines. She also was involved in the dinner talk. She was in a nursing-home, had done some cruising before and apparently enjoyed life on a cruise ship. Her family did not seem to have any problem with her being on the ship by herself. I think that is where she wanted to be and it was much cheaper than the cost of living in a nursing-home which also made it a good financial decision. I do not think she went ashore at all as I would see her in the casino playing the slot machines. Another older woman at the dinner table was a doctor from California, whose daughter was also a doctor. The other woman was from New York, and had done a lot of cruising with her husband who had passed on. She went on a cruise on her honeymoon when she got her first taste of some heavy seas, where all the luggage went sliding across the deck. That was before they had stabilizers on cruise ships. She talked about how good she was at spotting famous people in New York. I asked her if she is so good at recognizing famous people why did she not recognize me. I got the attention of the whole table for a while, until they figured out I was not famous! There were a lot of good times, or, as they would say over here, it was good crack.

When we arrived in Sydney, Australia, I said my goodbyes and told them how much I enjoyed their company and wished them smooth sailing the next three legs of the cruise. Another thing I noticed was there were a lot more ladies than men and the ship would give free passage to elderly men, who I would think were intended to be dance partners. For the ladies, they wore a badge that identified themselves.

We had an overnight in Sydney so I went ashore and booked my flight up to Bangkok and found a hotel for the next couple of nights. I really enjoyed Sydney, as I found the people very friendly. I found this to be true for anywhere which is isolated, and Australia is isolated way down under. I did find a hotel which had a casino, with a couple of crap (dice) tables. This is my game of choice, as I know the odds on any roll of a pair of dice. I can make my bets where I can get the odds down to 1.4 percent in the house favor which is low for casino games. It so happened I did have some great rolls and won a nice lump of money - it was nice to have a pocket full of Australian dollars to carry with me heading north to Thailand, where I had not been in over forty years. Somehow I thought Thailand was a bit closer to Australia. It was a long flight.

The daily poker players were also fun people; one married player was also planning his next trip. One woman poker player who was on the ship alone had a husband who was planning on joining the ship in Hong Kong for the second two legs of the trip. Another player was a retired Army officer who lived in Las Vegas and played poker a lot there with the same players who all knew each other well. He did say that when they got a new player as a visiting player it sort of changed the game and it was not as good. As a long time poker player I could understand that. The thing that surprised me was it was a pick up game and the ship had no part in it.

Thailand

When I landed in Thailand I made a phone call to a friend from Ireland and was pleasantly surprised he was there and answered. We had a short chat and I got in a taxi heading to Pattaya, Thailand - about a 2-hour cab ride to meet him at an apartment complex. He had another Irish friend with him who had a small flat to rent in that complex. So I was set up with a small completely furnished flat with a low monthly rent. It was not centrally located which was why the rent was low. Taxis are very cheap and easy to find, and there are also a lot of motor bike taxis for short trips. They also had pick-up trucks, fitted out with a bench on both sides of the bed, holding about 8-10 people, which ran along all the main streets, where you jump on and off anywhere just by pushing a button to let the driver know, and you go up to pay the driver about 25 cents. This mode of transport was a good fit for me as walking any distance started to become a bit troublesome. The first sign of ageing was where I was unable to walk the streets for hours, I really missed just walking up and down those little streets with all kinds of little businesses to explore. It wasn't long before I had the city pretty sorted out as to what was where. The air quality in the city was not the best. I noticed it more coming from north-west Ireland, right on the sea with a constant flow of fresh air off the Atlantic ocean. It was warm with a lot of sunshine through.

They also have a large tourism industry fed mostly by North Europeans. There were much fewer North American tourists. I would think distance from North America makes it more expensive and time-consuming to travel to Thailand for a short holiday. What they did have was a large Russian tourist invasion, which I have never been around before. This was the time frame when the price of oil was going through the roof, bringing a lot of dollars into Russia, and this fed the Russian section of the tourist trade. What I found out about this segment of the tourist trade was that the Thai and Russian governments put a few things into place to make the Russians' stay easier. A large hospital in Pattaya always had a Russian-speaking interpreter present at all times. All the Russian tourists had a document in the Thai language with a phone number to a Russian national who spoke Thai, to sort out any problems that involved the guards or police. I would think it would mostly be drink-related anti-social behavior - I became aware that some Russian tourists would order food off the menu, and if when it arrived it was not what they wanted, they would just walk out of the restaurant without paying their bill.

Thailand was a central hub point for tourists to plan other short trips to other places in the Far East. There were a lot of small travel agents shops that had some very cheap shorts trips. They advertised some all inclusive trips to Vietnam, and that was where I decided to go next.

Back to Vietnam

Thirty-nine years since I was evacuated from a US Army medical hospital by plane to Clark Air Force hospital in the Philippines, I purchased a flight and booked a hotel in Saigon (I still call it Saigon). It was a strange feeling landing in Vietnam, perhaps on the same air strip from which I was flown to the Philippines for more medical care. All the previous times I entered Vietnam it was always by ship, another first.

In the taxi I took from the airport to the hotel I had booked, the cab had a string of rosary beads hanging from the rear view mirror. The first thing I think of is how much influence the Catholic French had on the country before the US got involved in their civil war. I am always glad to see freedom of religion in a communist country. They can only do that by tweaking Karl Marx's writings. No longer those godless commies.

It was nice after thirty-nine years to be riding in a taxi around Saigon again, looking for my hotel. Here is another first, as all the times I had been to Vietnam, I had never stayed at a hotel before, it was always the ship. My first stay in a hotel in Vietnam was at a really pleasant hotel. I took a walk around the hotel district and was surprised to find so many nice European restaurants. I had dinner at the hotel where I was staying, and after dinner went to the bar to have a drink. English was understood and spoken by the staff. I asked where Nan Bay was, as I only remembered it was about ten miles south of Saigon on the Mekong river. The bartender put me on to a fellow patron in the bar by the name of Rick. Rick was an interesting story, as he was a Pole who emigrated with his family to Liverpool, England when in his teens. He was put into the school system with very little English to speak of. He told me it was not easy, but he got some help from, of all people, John Lennon, of the world's most famous band, the Beatles. He told me he still had letters from John. I did not ask to see them as I totally believed him. I told him my story of why I was back in Vietnam and where I was from and where I was living. We had a lot in common as he also spent time in Northern Ireland with the English army. We talked about the island of Ireland and he told me there was an Irish pub in Saigon and we went down there together, he knew all the staff. At this time he had been in Vietnam for close to twenty years and had a grown daughter there. His job in Vietnam was going anywhere in the country where there was a bomb dropped by US war planes during wartime that had not exploded, and he and another Vietnamese soldier would defuse the bomb. He brought smiles to the people who lived in the area where the bombs were found.

He was great company and he asked me if I would want to make a trip with him to defuse an unexploded bomb, and naturally, as the adventurer that I am, I said yes. He said I would have to meet him at 6am at a place called the super bowl. I questioned the name and he said there was no problem, as all the taxi drivers knew the place. I got there before six and found a place where I got a cup of coffee to go and wait for Rick. I was waiting there with my small travel bag and six o'clock came and went and I was still waiting. Rick showed up about a half hour late but I was still glad to see him. He had a Vietnamese soldier with him who was the driver by the name of Chong. His partner's English was not that good, so we did not have much of an exchange of thoughts. The unexploded bomb was found north of Saigon, close to a port that I have been to quite a few times. It was called Cam Ram Bay, a very deep-water harbor. It was now operated by the Russian Navy and used as a submarine base. Subs like deep-water ports. The spoils go to the victors.

I asked but he would not let me go to the bomb site for safety reasons, so I stayed at a strange place that had little cabins and a restaurant but few other guests. I do not believe this area was being used to promote tourism. I stayed there for two nights while Rick and Chong did their work to defuse the bomb, and hoped everything would go well to make it harmless and dispose of the explosives materials. Those big bombs had a lot of explosive materials and I asked Rick if the explosive material was then used to make other bombs; he said he knows what happens and it is not used to make more bombs. Perhaps firecrackers. It was the first time that I had traveled up Route One which was north and south along the coast, as I always traveled north or south along the Mekong River before. The trip back to Saigon was good, and I got to know Rick a bit better.

Another trip I made with Rick and his partner was to the southern end of the Mekong Delta as far as the Cambodia border. The large area south and west of Saigon is known as the rice bowl of the far east. Perfect conditions for the cultivation of rice. No way could that area be patrolled as it has so many waterways with so many small boats doing what they do. I cannot remember the name of the city we went to, but it was rather large. I know they had some islands off the coast that were being promoted by Vietnam as tourist islands that had ferry service from the mainland to the islands. I went down to the ferry port the next morning to get a ferry over to check out the islands. But I got to the dock and was told the weather was bad and there was no ferry service on that day. I was a bit disappointed, as I was interested in seeing the islands - they were under dispute with Cambodia as to ownership. There was a lot of tension at this particular border crossing with Cambodia. The tension has been there for a few years since Cambodia was invaded by the Vietnam army during the horror reign of

Pol Pot in Cambodia where thousands if not hundreds of thousands were murdered in ethnic cleansing.

I also knew that when you live in a country for years, your values and thinking evolve to be the same as the ones born there. Rick and Chong both had problems with Vietnamese who migrated to the States and did well and received their US passports and came back as tourists, when they flaunted their wealth in a way that the ones who stayed and were still very poor found offensive. I could understand that, and I could also understand why they wanted to come home to see their families, and they did not want to come home with their tails between their legs. I know in Ireland if you go to live abroad and come back for a visit, you are expected to spend money like a drunken sailor.

I was glad I did make the trip back after so many years, to see how much the country had improved, and it was great to see the difference in the life of a country that peace makes. It was the same when I got back to Ireland after the peace agreement was signed in Northern Ireland.

Having got back to South Vietnam, I thought it would be nice to travel to North Vietnam. Being a train buff, I found they had a train from Saigon to Hanoi, It was about a thirty five hour trip through the heart of the country. All my time before was along the coast line up as far north as Danang which was close to the demilitarized zone. I went to the main Saigon train station and booked my return ticket with a soft class sleeper for the over 1000-mile train trip. The train I booked departed close to midnight and arrived in Hanoi early morning on the third day. It was an older train, and from talking to Rick, I gathered the train was not that modern and even the soft class was not that soft. It takes a lot to keep me away from train travel. I got to the train station and I could see how it was a full train with mostly the lower class passengers. They did serve you food in the soft class sleeper car. They had four bunks in there, and the bottom bunk was more expensive than the upper bunk. My ticket was for a lower bunk, and inside the sleeper room it was pretty tight. Anyhow, I laid down on my bed with the most expensive ticket possible. After the train left the station, it was time to get some shut-eye. The bed was comfortable enough and I did get some sleep. Early the next morning the train pulled into the Danang station, which is the last stop before the DMZ zone. Going through the DMZ there were some of the best views I have ever seen, going through tunnels and round bends with unbelievable views. I was amazed how well the track line was built in such hostile conditions. I would think it was built during the French occupation. After about three hours we arrived in Hue. North of there, apart from the train station towns, there were a lot of rice paddies, buffaloes and rice farmers. There was a whole day on the train plus another night before arriving in Hanoi in the early morning. I got a cab to the hotel I had booked and I had to wake up the night porter to open the door. It was nice to get into bed and get a few more hours of sleep. Rick gave me an address of another Irish pub in Hanoi that I went to the next two nights. I had some Irish music news articles that I left there. I took a good look around the hotel district and found some places to eat, but not as good as the ones in Saigon. And Hanoi is no way as large as Saigon.

I spent three days there, and it was a fun time. I was glad I got to experience the Vietnam rail system. It was really great scenery both in the north and south.

Thailand

When I got back to Thailand I settled in for the winter. Anytime you travel abroad you have to be aware of what visas are required. Each country has its own rules, which can be complex, as each has hundreds of different visas which can change anytime. When I arrived back in Thailand I got another thirty-day permission to stay on my visa. It can be expensive if you, for whatever reason, let it expire without leaving the country, or get another visa without leaving the country.

This was a busy tourist time for Thailand. so I got to chat with many other visitors and some permanent residents who had been there for years. Some I talked to said they were considering making Cambodia their new place to reside for financial reasons. Thailand is the richest of all the border countries in that area. Because of that, they also have a lot of immigrants, legal and illegal, crossing the border for better work opportunities. The cause of the migration into Thailand is that it has a sound economy with tourism, auto assembly plants, manufacturing plus they export a lot of rice.

My time was getting short on my visa so I had to start to plan my exit so i could enter again. To leave so you can come back in sounds a bit silly. I would think that the government has a good reason for this rule, otherwise they would change it, as there were a lot of people like myself who wished to stay in Thailand for longer than thirty days. They did have a scheduled bus service direct to the Cambodia border where you could exit Thailand and enter Cambodia and immediately turn around and re-enter Thailand on the same bus, with a new 30-day visa stamp in your passport which cost 20.00 dollars. You had to make a reservation to board the Mimi bus at 6am, get to the border about 10am and return about 4 pm, to the same place you boarded the bus at 6am. The cost of the bus ticket there was a stop scheduled for a meal on the return ride. I only did that trip one time, as I qualified for a pensioner's visa which could be renewed every three months in Pattaya.

After about four months I got sick with gallbladder stones and spent seven days in a Thai government hospital; it was an experience to spend time in a third world country hospital. It was a teaching hospital, so you did have a lot of student doctors and nurses which is always good to see. After I got discharged from the hospital, I was still feeling a bit weak, so I stayed for about a week and then decided I could make the trip back to Ireland for June and July, 2008. I stayed in Ireland for about two months, then headed back to Thailand. I also had my pensioner's visa in order. After I got back to Thailand I stayed for a while in the condo that was not so close to the beach, but then I found another flat closer to the beach, much easier to get around and no more taxis. It was right across the street from a big Tesco supermarket which was nice, with a good stock of western foods.

The Cadillac LaSalle auto club that I had belonged to since 1986 was having a grand national annual meet in early August for three days, which I wanted to get to, as there were many club members I had not seen for years and I wanted to catch up on their revolving auto collection of Cadillacs and LaSalles. I departed Thailand in July for Ireland and spent a month there before boarding the QE2, the newest of the Queen Elisabeth class ships - it was a direct crossing from Southampton to New York, returning on the same ship next trip back to Southampton. That gave me about two weeks to get to the three-day car show and meet. I also made a trip down to Florida for a short visit with my brother, Joe. It was a good two weeks, and then I was back on board the QE2 headed back to Southampton, England, and on to Ireland for a bit of time before heading back to Thailand for the winter. It was a nice ship with fine crew and officers. On this trip to Thailand I did get my documents for my pensioner's visa. No more 6 am small bus trips to the Cambodia border.

Thailand 2008-9

I stayed over in Thailand from September through early February, when I was on my way back to Ireland and on to the States for a trip down to Florida. I stopped by to see brother John and sister Helen in New Jersey. I talked to John to see if he would like to do a transatlantic from Fort Lauderdale, Fl. to Dublin, with a stop in Bermuda, the Canaries islands and Scotland, and on to Dublin, where we could disembark and I could go up to Donegal, and he could fly back home to New Jersey. He was very interested as it had been a long time since he was on a deep-water ship. When he was much younger he worked on oil tankers for a few years running the east coast to Texas and a few trips down to South America and the Caribbean so he was well used to the sea. The sailing date was in mid-April, we made arrangements that I would pick him up at the Orlando, Fla. airport and we would spend a few days with Joe, and me and him would make the three-hour drive south to Fort Lauderdale and board the ship for the crossing.

The trip with John was different than Joe's. I asked if he wanted a table with four, six or eight? He wanted a table for two for whatever reason I do not know. So we had our table and every night it was good service and food. Towards the end of the trip the waiter asked if we were married, I guess he thought we were a gay couple. They had a good bridge card game on that trip where there was another American who was my partner. He had been living in Germany for many years. He served in the US Army and after he was discharged he decided to live and work in Germany. When we got to Scotland, John for some reason stayed aboard the ship, and I went ashore and got some nice wool sweaters as gifts for him to take back for my sister Helen's grandkids. I showed them to John and he said he should have gone ashore. We docked in Dublin early the next morning and we took a taxi to the airport where John had time to get his plane connection back home and I got the airport bus back to Donegal.

I stayed in Donegal until October when I found another reposition cruise to get back to Thailand by way of the Suez canal. I decided to enjoy the summer in Donegal. They have the annual Carrigart show. It is really a great car and tractor show, and the flea market they have is also very good with a great collection of stuff. This one-yearly show raises enough funds to finance the club for the entire year. I also noticed a trend of spending less and less time in Donegal. This was causing problems with Finbarr who was a great dog. My neighbor was getting very attached to him, so together we decided that it would be better for Finbarr that his neighbor's home would be his home, and he would not be a guest anymore. I very much enjoyed Finnbar's company when I was back in Donegal, but it would have been selfish of me to continue my ownership. It was a hard decision, but I loved him so much that I really thought it would be a good decision for his well-being.

2009-10

To get back to Thailand I found another Royal Caribbean ship that I had cruised on a previous relocation before, the Legend of the Seas. The Legend of the Seas was relocating this time from the summer in Europe to Singapore and China by way of the Suez Canal. I had to book back-to-back cruises, the first one was from Rome, Italy to Dubai, UAE, a twelve day trip and the second was thirteen days from Dubai to Singapore.

I booked my flight from Dublin to Rome for the 23rd of October. From the airport to the main port for Rome is about a three-hour bus ride. It was nice to be back aboard the Legend of the Seas for another trip. I found a nice table for dinner, which was all bridge players, with the director and her assistant. Our waiter, who was from Chile, was also setting up the bridge tables, which he got overtime pay for, I would think. During one of our dinner conversations, I found that the bridge assistance director was also a nun who left the religious life to get married and have children, and there was a waiter who was also into the monastic training for the priesthood, when he also left the religious life for whatever reason. The two of them had something that they could share. All together it was a twenty-five day cruise. It is always great to traverse the Suez canal. It is so different from the Panama canal. It was the French who built the Suez canal, before they tried to build a canal through Panama. The distance from France and widespread tropical sickness was just too much for them, and they quit. Panama has a large freshwater lake in the center. The ships go through locks that lift them up to the lake, and locks to lower them down to continue on to the ocean. The Pacific ocean is six inches higher than the Atlantic ocean which makes the locks a necessity. You also pass one ship at a time while you travel the canal in a convoy, with many ships traveling at a speed of 8 knots. The Suez canal is not wide enough for two way traffic, so to keep traffic moving in two directions, they have anchorages dug out of the side of the canal where ships can drop the hook and let the opposite moving convoy traffic pass.

After we passed through the canal, our first port was Dubai where we had an overnight stay. I took a taxi downtown. The taxi driver was from Pakistan and he said most all taxi drivers are from there. While on the ship, I had also been chatting with a husband and wife from India, who had been living in Dubai for over twenty years. He had three daughters born over there that he was raising. He was an accountant and I asked him if he could ever become a citizen of Dubai, UAE, his answer was very direct: never, nor his daughters. I felt him to be a fine gentleman, and I asked him and his wife if their marriage was an arranged marriage, and his wife lied to me and said no. It was later that I was talking to him and he told me it was an arranged marriage. So I would think his wife thought that people from the west think badly about arranged marriages for whatever reason. I have no problem with any marriage and always hope they work out well for all. The two of them had found very much in common.

The cruise ended in Singapore but as I was going to Thailand I disembarked in Phuket. There was no dock for the ship in Phuket so I had to get my luggage off the ship on to a small ferry to get to a dock and unload the luggage on to a small pier and a long walk to where I could get a taxi to a hotel. I stayed for a few days, a really nice place to tour, before booking a flight back to the small but nice Pattaya airport, where I knew more people.

I was back in Thailand and stayed until after the Christmas and New year holidays. While over there this trip, I did meet a lovely lady whose company I enjoyed. I gave her my brother Joe's phone that she could call. Having returned to Ireland after the holidays, I stopped by Donegal to check on the house and talk to my caretaker and read my post that was waiting there for me. I stayed down at the house and Finbarr knew I was back. The neighbor kept him in a closed outside shed, but he got out during the night and came down to my house and started to bark and bark. He wanted in the house but I did not let him in, as I was only going to be there for a week. I really wanted to let him in, but I thought it best not to.

CHAPTER 5 - NEW FAMILY

It had been a while since I had been down to see my friends in Costa Rica, so in February 2010, I decided to do another trip over to Florida to see how brother Joe was doing living by himself since his wife passed away. There was another gentleman who was also making a trip back to Florida, so we booked a ticket on the same day.

I spent about a week with Joe and then booked a flight down to Costa Rica. It was nice to get back to my old stomping grounds for a visit. I then booked a ship that was relocating back to Florida from Colon, Panama to Florida and on to California to do the summer cruises to Alaska for the summer. Time for another first when I boarded the Royal Caribbean Enchantment of the Seas in Limon, Costa Rica, for an eight-day cruise north to arrive in Florida on 19 April 2010, with a few stops in other Caribbean ports. I had been in and out of Costa Rica to Florida many times, but always through the airport in San Jose. While back with Joe in Florida, I found another Royal Caribbean ship Adventure of the Seas, relocating for a thirteen-day transatlantic crossing, departing May 2nd from San Juan, Puerto Rico onward, to arrive at Barcelona Spain May 15th. We made a few stops in the Caribbean and the Canary islands. While I had been staying with brother Joe, the phone rang and Joe answered the phone 'hello', and the response was 'hello, darling'. I was sitting next to him and I saw the strange look on his face. Joe does not get too many phone calls, so this was a strange one. I think his response was 'who do you want to talk to?' and the other end said 'is this not Barney?'.
That is when he passed the phone to me, and she said I sound just like my brother - which is true, as my brother was once called a liar, because the party on the other end was sure it was me.

Anyhow it was a very important phone call as she told me she was pregnant and she wanted me to know, and see if and when I was coming back to Thailand. She was no longer in Pattaya and was living in the country with her mother and young nephew. I asked how she was feeling, and said I would be back. I already had my passage booked on the Adventure of the Seas to arrive in Barcelona, Spain on 15th May, from there I had to get back to Donegal, and there I would book passage back to Bangkok. I was glad she was feeling well and in a good place, which I was happy for. I knew this was going to be a life-changing event for me and her, and I was anxious to get back to Thailand. I just got busy with thinking about the mystery of life. The next year, 2010, was going to be exciting. Little did I know that this would also be the last time I would see and enjoy time with my brother and best friend.

    I arrived in Bangkok airport in early June and was met by Mam and her cousin with a small car. She was now in her third semester and had a big bump. We traveled back to Pattaya and went back to the same accommodations where we stayed before I left for Donegal. There were a lot of the same guests there and they gave me a great welcome back. We only stayed there a month and then rented a house with a six-month lease; Mam's sister Gaib decided to join us there, as there was an extra bedroom, and she got a job close by and was able to help Mam with wee Bridget. It was an area outside the town center and far from the beach, of mostly middle class Thais and a few Europeans. This was the first house I lived in while in Thailand, and that was the house we were living in when Bridget was born.

    Bridget was a caesarean birth, so it occurred just when the doctor said was the right time. She picked a date of 2 November 2010. It was not an easy birth for Mam, she had to stay in the hospital for seven days and I had a real fear of losing her. Every day I went to the hospital to visit. It was a ward with eight beds and all the new mothers that were there when she joined the ward were discharged, new mothers appeared and were discharged and Mam was still there. This was my third time going through this, the other two ended very quickly, one being twenty-seven days and the other a miscarriage after four months.

    On the seventh day we brought her home where we stayed until the lease was up, and then we made a trip back to Ireland to show Bridget to all of the neighbors. At this time we had two marriage ceremonies, one with the Thai family and the other to register our marriage in Thailand. We sorted out Bridget's country of birth registration at the US and Irish embassies. The US Embassy had doubts as to whether Mam was her real mother and perhaps she was using Bridget to get a US visa. It was a long process which took a lot of time and a thousand dollars. First we had to go to the hospital and register with the hospital using our ID papers, so the hospital could use their doctor to do the test. We also had to use a US lab approved by the embassy where they shipped the lab kit directly to the embassy. Mam, Bridget and myself were given an appointment at the embassy, where we were escorted to the inner circle with a large table with the doctor from the Thai hospital, plus the embassy personnel with the test kit. The three of us took the test, witnessed and signed documents. The test kit was repackaged and signed and sealed and then sent back to the lab in the USA for testing for the embassy. The lab sent the positive results back to the embassy and ourselves, and she was granted US Citizenship. The Irish embassy was no problem as they just gave her Irish papers with no problem. Bridget also got herself a Thai passport and ID identification number. So when she was very young we did make a few trips up to Bangkok for documents.

Death of my brother Joe

It was during this period that my brother Joseph took sick over in Florida ; he had no family there, I was the one closest to him and always made a point of stopping by to see him when I was in the area. I talked to him every day and he told me what was happening. What happened was the meals-on-wheels delivery driver found him on the floor when he delivered the meal. He helped him up and put him in his chair and my brother said he was alright. The driver went next door and told the resident to check on him later. Later the neighbor came by and found him on the floor again and called an ambulance to take him to the hospital.

He did have a few lady friends who would always stop by to spend some time with him and do what they could for him. Once a week they always took him out for a philly cheese steak sandwich. So he had their phone number and they went to see him and did what they could. The medics did a lot of testing and came back with cancer of the liver, which is not good. He told me about what they found, and they also told him that they could operate but the chances of a successful outcome were not good. They also told him liver cancer is a fast mover, so he decided not to be operated on. He went to a rehab center to see if he could get back to where he could walk and go back home. He never did get well enough to go home again. The lady that I knew from my visits was holding his hand when he passed away.

I talked to her and the owner of the trailer camp-ground who I also knew from my visit, and told him to let the ladies take what they want. On one of my visits down there, Joe wanted me to go and get my name also on the trailer which I did, and he showed me where he kept the paper. From talking to Joe on a regular basis I knew the owner did not come around for well over a year to collect the rent. So I called him up and told him where the paper was. He found the paper and posted it over to me in Thailand and I signed it and sent it back to him to do what he wanted with the trailer.

I also talked to the two ladies, who I believe really loved him. I just told them to sort out his worldly belongings, which were very modest, as best they could. They arranged for his cremation and told me the info and I got in touch with the crematorium and they told me the cost. They told me I could not pay unless I had proof I was his brother. I asked how I could do that when I was over here in Thailand. They told me I would have to go to the American embassy and get a document with a seal stating that I am who I say I am and send it over to them, and then they would be able to accept payment from me. That meant a days journey up to Bangkok and paying fifty dollars for the seal and document and posting it off to them. That was done, and when I called, they had received the notarized paper and took my credit card info and proceeded with the cremation. His ashes were picked up by the same lady who was holding his hand when he passed on. She made a trip down to the Florida Keys and put the ashes in the sea. He liked to talk about the great trip him and his wife of many years made down to the Keys. He was not only my brother but also my best friend. May he rest in peace.

Bridget was a healthy baby with a bit of colic, but other than that she was good. When Bridget was about six months we decided to make a trip with her back to Ireland. It was around the end of May when Mam and Bridget got their visas for the visit. With Bridget being Irish and Mam being my wife they both got six months, plenty of time to sort their papers out when we got over there. She was concerned about the cost of living in Ireland and my small pension which is understandable. When it was just me and Finnbar over in Ireland, it was enough, but with a family it fell quite a bit short. We stayed for three months and got Bridget's papers with the papers we brought from the Thailand government and the Ireland consul in Bangkok. With those papers we got Bridget's foreign birth registered with the Irish Foreign office and she received her Irish citizenship papers.

Mam found a Thai lady who had also married an Irishman, who lived down the road not far away. It was a good one, as they became friends and in turn Mam made some connections with the Thai community in the local area. She also found out where the Asian food shops were located.

We stayed for just three months, as this was Mam's longest time ever out of Thailand, she missed her family and friends over there, she was homesick. With the cost of living over in Ireland and our funds getting low. we decided to book a flight back to Thailand.

When we arrived back in Thailand, we went back to the same place as before the house rental. It was nice to be back with old friends in the complex. We got a room on the first floor end room, with a window with a view. We had to pick up a few items to cook and do laundry. This place was a really nice complex where they had short-term guests and longer term ones like ourselves. This is where Bridget had her first birthday party, with a good turn-out of guests. There were also some other guests who had older kids. Then there was another couple, a Belgium gentleman who had a Thai wife and a young son about the same age as Bridget. So there was a good mix of guests and great security. This is also the place where Bridget passed her second birthday.

This was a nice period for us but as time went on and Bridget was now two, we decided to try Ireland again. Mam had kept in touch with her Thai friend from the village that was still there. The three of us arrived back in our home village of Carrigart with a nice welcome back from all. We settled in and Mam decided to become a resident and reported to the local garda station to register and show her papers. They did have a special guard there who sorted all the immigrant papers out. Mam had to make an appointment with the guard every three months to get a stamp in her passport plus she also had an ID card that she carried with her all the time. This trip we applied for government assistance. The way things were going at the end of every month, there was less in our reserve funds than the month before, so it would have just been time before we could not put food on the table. The government was very good and evaluated the situation with the numbers and my US pension, and awarded us an income supplement which made it possible for us to live in Ireland.

When it came to August and time for school to open, we knew they had a pre-school called Rainbow, but did not know what the age requirement was. We got in touch and found out Bridget was old enough to go to the first year of pre-school in 2013. Bridget took to school like a duck to water. At this time my sister Helen came over for a visit and was with us the first day of Bridget's school. Before the first day of school we took Bridget up to the Rainbow school for a look around. So when we got to the school on her first day, she could not get into school fast enough. Helen was very impressed with how brave she was. We have been here ever since and Carrigart is the only school system she knows. Little did I know there would be another 2nd surprise in September 2014 when Mam was pregnant again. The baby was due to arrive in June 2015.

Bridget was coming up to five years old and she had never been introduced to my family in the United States. So I started looking at my favorite cruise vacations site, to look for any cruise ships doing a relocation to the US in late 2014. I found one 16-night cruise from Barcelona to New Orleans, Louisiana, aboard the Royal Caribbean ship Serenade of the Seas. The departure date from Barcelona, Spain, was sixth of November to arrive in New Orleans on November 22nd. This would be my first cruise since before Bridget was born. This would also be the first cruise for Mam and Bridget. There was a bit of excitement in the house planning the trip. From New Orleans to Philadelphia, I booked a train ticket on the Amtrak railroad system with a sleeper berth for us, as this was to be a twenty-five hour train ride. I also booked the air flight back from Newark, New Jersey to Dublin, Ireland.

When I was putting this trip together, I called my cousin David in New Jersey, as he had already made a few crossings on relocating ships, to see if he wanted to make the trip. I told him he could fly over and stay with us until it was time to fly to Barcelona to board the Serenade of the Seas. He said he would like to make the trip with us, so he was included in all the bookings as far as Philadelphia, where there would be a car rental waiting to take David back home to New Jersey, close by where my brother John and sister Helen lived. On the ship booking, David had his own cabin. On the train, David and myself had one cabin, and Mam and Bridget had theirs. We all shared a large hotel room in New Orleans waiting for the day the train departed. This was all done from my chair and phone from the hills of Donegal.

On the 6th of November we departed from Carrigart to Letterkenny for a bus ride to the airport for our plane to Barcelona. We boarded the ship, found our cabins and settled in for the cruise. From Barcelona we headed south for the warm weather, and stopped first in the Canary Islands and picked up the southern trade winds for the Caribbean islands. We stopped off at a few islands and made it around the southernmost Florida Keys island into the Gulf of Mexico, steering a course for New Orleans. Royal Caribbean cruise lines do have activities for children, more so than most cruise lines, just as the Holland American line specializes in elderly passengers with their well-developed health center. I did play in the bridge games and we went to some of the dinners, but mostly did the self-service cafeteria food courts, as there were four of us doing different activities. The time window was good and more choices. We all took advantage of all the port calls and got ashore for some sightseeing. Mam got to know two ladies from Australia that she still keeps in contact with. I myself would like to make one more trip with Brendan but that is questionable.

I think we all enjoyed the long train ride up to Philadelphia. It was great to see brother John and sister Helen and visit a few nieces and nephews as it was the first time they met Bridget. The last visit we made was to my nephew Charles, up in the Poconos mountains in Pennsylvania, which was close to the Newark airport for our flight back to Ireland. Bridget missed a few weeks of her pre-school but I think the trip was worth it. We were back in Ireland for the Christmas holidays.

Things went well with Mam's second pregnancy. This being Mam's second child, she was able to compare the prenatal care and maternity care at the hospitals in both Thailand and Ireland. Her conclusion was that Ireland was much better, and Brendan was born on 2nd of June 2015. We were not long back from the hospital with Brendan when we had to get some work done on the house, and we had to find some temporary accommodations not far away for ten days while the work was being done. After a few days Mam took sick with appendicitis and was hospitalized while still nursing him. So Brendan had to go to the hospital with his mother while she had her appendix taken out. The whole intense episode took about four or five days.

With Bridget and Brendan, it was now time to get a dog. Bridget was asking to get a pet. My next neighbor down the road had Springer spaniels with pups and the timing was perfect, as they were seven weeks old coming up to her birthday. So I went down and picked a pup and went back and gave him to her as her fifth birthday present. With wee baby Brendan and Jack the new puppy, Mam said it was like having two babies. To say the least, it was interesting times in this ole homestead.

During this time period another interesting relationship was in the works. I got an email from one of my nieces, Cindy, who was involved in these ancestry DNA web sites. She got an email from a lady who was also involved in these search sites, who was interested in Cindy's DNA chart as it was very close to her own chart. A few emails went back and forth. It so happened that my niece's grandfather and great-grandfather were both from the same area in Ireland. Maureen had been searching for many years for her biological father. Cindy told her that her mother had four brothers. Maureen asked my niece if she could find out their blood types to see if they would match. She sent me another email and asked if I could help. I told her my type and my brother John's type. Neither of them matched and my other brother had already passed away and I had no way of finding his blood type out. He did leave behind three sons who did not want to know if they had a half-sister.

Maureen had been adopted by an Irish couple in Pennsylvania who still had their parents living in Ireland, not too far from where I was living. She spent her summer holidays with her grandparents in Ireland and also studied the Irish language. She wanted to plan a trip over to Ireland to visit her adoptive Irish family and wanted to come up to see me with a visit. She did get to meet another of my nieces, Laura, and the three of them had a few get-togethers, as Laura's husband was also adopted, and they exchanged some info on tracking biological parents. So, I said I would gladly meet her to find out her story. I picked her up in early May 2019 from the bus station and brought her home and she met my daughter Bridget, son Brendan and wife Mam. Maureen stayed about three days and we exchanged a few stories about our Irish connections. She was with her new family with two daughters and husband and one granddaughter. I very much enjoyed her visit.

When she got back home to her family, the girls had another get-together, and my niece, Laura had a spare DNA test kit; and she also had a trip planned for Ireland with her and her brother, Eddie, and their families, ten in all. She asked me if I would take a DNA test and I said yes, to give Maureen closure with this line of her search.

Laura arrived in Ireland with her own family and her brother's family in late June 2019, and they had a good tour of the country, before they all reached way up north of the country, where I am. It was really great to meet them all when they arrived. Mam put a nice spread of Thai food out for them and after a long day's drive it was enjoyed by all. As this was their first trip to Ireland, we talked about the local area and some good tourist attractions in Donegal. I gave them directions to their hotel, and they decided to take Bridget with them on the tours they had planned for their few days in Donegal. The day before their planned departure, we all had a great meal at a restaurant picked by my niece, a place where my nearest neighbor worked. I called my neighbor who made the reservation for fourteen. When they were leaving out the next day they stopped to say goodbye, and I took the DNA test. I also called my friend who had a small museum on the road out of town and asked him to open up for my visitors, so they could take a tour of how the Irish lived a hundred years ago and the furniture they had. It also showed the old fireplace with the pots and kettle all in place and the chairs around the fire place. During that period the fire never went out. Whoever was the first up got the fire going from the ashes for the new day, to get the kettle hot enough to make the first pot of tea. They were very impressed by my friend's place on their last day in Donegal.

They had one more night in Dublin and flew home the next day, in early July.

About a week went by and I got an email from Laura, who said the test came back positive. A HAPPY END TO THE CLOSE OF THE SEARCH. I was a bit surprised because of the blood type. My biological daughter came into the world in 1965 when I was in the US Army stationed at Fort Story, Virginia, and I would make weekend trips up to Philadelphia when I had a week-end pass. I believe these homes for unwed mothers at that time made it hard for adoptees to find their biological parents, so they gave false information. So, I believe the DNA test to be correct and a mistake was made with the blood type.

So that was the third good surprise - me and Maureen still keep in touch, and she was very happy to know she has a half-brother and sister living in Ireland, a country she loves and whose language she speaks.

When I started writing these memoirs it was for the first good surprise, Bridget, who is just ten. It was not long before the second good surprise, Brendan, made himself known. Then out of the blue my niece got an email from a stranger, who turned out to be my biological daughter, who is a wonderful person and has had a good life with her own good family. I think this is a good time to put these memoirs to rest and enjoy the rest of my life on earth. I really did enjoy writing these pages to pass on to my three children and anyone else who would enjoy my life stories. With love to Bridget, Brendan and the oldest and most settled, Maureen. **From your Father, Barney.**

****

Barney's Family

Aunt Annie at her cottage in Donegal, 2000

Barney and Bridget, 2019

Barney, Mam and Brendan, 2019

Barney, Bridget and Brendan, 2019

Barney's new-found daughter, Maureen, with her granddaughter

ACKNOWLEDGEMENTS

I want to give thanks to many people in my life, some of whom are part of the stories in this book:
Special thanks to the following families:
Mister Leslie (Sorrows) Williams and his sons, who were very much into sport and who contributed great help and enthusiasm.
Don Carlos Mora and his son Tony, my good friend, who helped me many times, and who was a a great help to my nephew Chuck with his computer school project for many years.
The McLeod family with Daniel and all his kids, in all my sports activities and other work.
The Mullins, who were a great sporting family, including Buddie their father whose kids thrived in sports. Also, his son Rickie, and my good friend Rogelio and his uncle, by the same name.
The Cunninghams who were the keepers of the sporting equipment and the sports pitch. They were a great help as a family and kids.
Mr. Spencer who I will always remember with a smile on my face. He also had the best fish camp down on the white beach, and the best fishing knowledge of the local and coastal areas. His sons also took an active interest in all sports.
I cannot forget the help from the Jehovah's Witness family from the white beach area of Cahuita, along with my first and great fishing partners Arnold, Nitch, Pete Ferguson. The support by their entire family will forever be appreciated.
Martin Luther, with all eight sons and especially Eduardo who was a great help to his mother, as she was a fine coconut oil maker and loved to play her chance numbers.
Mr. Fred Ferguson and Mr. Seller Johnson for their help with my horses.
Mr. Palmer and his family.
I would also like to give special thanks to all who assisted my nephew Chuck Moore on his mission with his computer school in Cahuita for over six years. Special thanks to Mr. Todd Scotland and Mr. Tony Mora for their support during that time.

In another context, to the parents of the Killian family who adopted my biological daughter, Maureen, I would like to express my eternal gratitude for the wonderful way you raised my biological daughter during those very important formative years to become who she is today.

And finally, special thanks to Anne Barlow, her sister Anupam Barlow and Isabelle Gouzou for all their devoted work on editing and laying out the raw material of this book and helping to get this long drawn out project across the finish line and on to the printers.

The picture on the back cover is of my parents in Villas, NJ in the mid-1960s.

BARNEY CARR

Printed in Great Britain
by Amazon